THE POWER OF ONE

The Ed McAteer Story

ISBN #0-9753725-0-5

Printed in the United States of America.

THE POWER OF ONE

The Ed McAteer Story

Foreword by Howard Phillips

Thomas Lindberg   Jonathan Lindberg   Daniel E. Johnson

"Life must be lived forwards
but can only be understood backwards."

-Kierkegaard

TABLE OF CONTENTS

DEDICATION

To

Faye

John and Wendy Beckett

Nina Katz

Jack Belz

FOREWORD

Ed McAteer merits the respect and appreciation of all patriotic Americans and Christians throughout the world. Ed has been a faithful and cheerful exponent of God's word, and has made extraordinary personal sacrifices to fulfill his calling.

It was my privilege to meet Ed in the mid-1970s. By God's grace, I was able to secure the participation of Ed McAteer in the work of The Conservative Caucus, which he served as National Field Director for several years until he left The Caucus to pursue his work through the Religious Roundtable.

Although many others have claimed the credit, it was Ed McAteer who had the vision to perceive and launch what came to be known as the "Religious Right."

I shall always remember the day on which Ed and I drove to Lynchburg, Virginia, to share Ed's vision with Dr. Jerry Falwell who, at Ed's encouragement, launched the Moral Majority. In Ed's company, it was my privilege to meet literally dozens of Christian clergy and lay leaders who caught Ed's vision and made a profound difference in the elections of 1978 and 1980.

Many people rightly believe that the event that Ed organized in the fall of 1980 at Reunion Arena in Dallas, provided the fulcrum for Ronald Reagan's Presidential candidacy in which millions of Christians were mobilized to reject the born-again incumbent, Jimmy Carter, in favor of the McAteer-endorsed Ronald Reagan.

Ed has taken part in some of the key battles of the latter part of the Twentieth Century, including opposition to the Panama Canal treaties, to President Carter's socialized medicine schemes, fighting the Carter-Brezhnev SALT treaty, as well as helping launch support for what came to be known as the

Strategic Defense Initiative, and much more.

Ed's loyalty and friendship is something I have always cherished, and which has been a consistent source of encouragement and inspiration. Ed and his wonderful wife Faye and his family have truly made a difference in America.

I pray that for many generations to come, Ed McAteer will be recognized for his historic achievements in Christ's service.

Howard Phillips
President
The Conservative Caucus

Ed McAteer

An eyewitness of His majesty

CHAPTER 1

DALLAS

It felt like the ground was shifting that day in Texas, late in August 1980, when thousands of religious leaders decided to get involved in the political process. Leading the charge were a former marketing executive and Baptist layman from Memphis and a dynamic 31-year-old evangelist from Ft. Worth.

Religious Roundtable founder and president, E.E. "Ed" McAteer organized and was chairman of the now-famous National Affairs Briefing held at Reunion Arena in Dallas. Roundtable vice president, James Robison, described it as "something God put on my heart." Former Gov. Ronald Reagan was the keynote speaker. The event drew 20,000 people, including 5,000 pastors, priests and rabbis, 400 journalists, 200 media outlets including all three major TV networks, BBC, Scandinavian Broadcasting Company, *Time* and *Newsweek*, the *Washington Post* and the *New York Times*.

The list of speakers included Jesse Helms, Phil Crane, Tim LaHaye, Jerry Falwell, Pat Robertson, Phyllis Schlafly, Howard Phillips, Paul Weyrich, Adrian Rogers, James Kennedy, McAteer and Robison, not to mention Reagan.

The time was right for such an event. America was still

feeling the sting of recent attacks on long-held practices and beliefs. Nine black-robed, unelected jurists, arrogantly flying in the face of 200 years of tradition, had struck down prayer and Bible reading in the schools and declared the Ten Commandments to be offensive and unfit for schoolchildren; permissible in the closet perhaps, but not in public.

If this judicial power grab shook the rafters in the Sixties, the *Roe v. Wade* decision in 1973 sent shockwaves that threatened to bring the whole house down.

Millions of Americans were tired of it. Tired of abortion on demand and politicians who lied about it. Many of them claimed to oppose the procedure but insisted on "a woman's right to choose." In defending their indefensible position, they said abortion should be "safe, legal, and rare." The death toll reached 4,000 a day — precious, little, God-created infants, deliberately dismembered and slain in clinics, where the lethal practice was neither safe, legal, nor rare.

One senator affirmed, "I am pro-values, pro-faith, pro-family, and pro-choice" — until language has no meaning.

Parents were tired of the secularization of education. They had had it with college professors who made no effort to hide their hatred of Christianity or their contempt for the country that gave them a platform (and salary) to preach that hate. They were fed up with the imposition of gay rights on every level of society and the use of the First Amendment to protect pornographers and perverts while imposing laws that restricted the influence of those who have religious convictions.

What was going on here?

"The First Amendment, which was intended to preserve religious rights," noted Chicago pastor Erwin Lutzer, "is used to deny Christians the freedom to be involved in the national debate. Christian bashing in movies, sitcoms, and talk shows has become popular and commonplace. So successful has the media been in defining America that most people believe it is the Christians who want to impose their values on society, without realizing that the liberals have been doing so for decades. We are now portrayed as villains whose patriotic duty is best served by keeping our opinions to ourselves."

Why are evangelicals ignored in the marketplace? Why does their voice not matter? Why are they the enemy? "The average fundamentalist felt alienated from the mainstream of American culture," said Robison. Millions of Christians believed that their return to the cultural debate was long overdue, so when the call came they packed their bags and headed for Dallas. Leading political leaders were invited to appear and address the issues that were important to people of faith.

Both Jimmy Carter and independent candidate John Anderson had declined the invitation. McAteer made a point of extending an invitation to the President in a private meeting with one of his aides. The response was less than encouraging. "Ed," the aide said, "I don't think the President would be interested in participating in the beauty contest." Carter, the "born-again" candidate, had won the presidency with strong support from the faithful but lost favor when he failed to appoint evangelicals to key positions, waffled on abortion, and generally failed to support positions that Christians considered important.

Anderson emphasized the personal nature of his faith, kept most religious leaders at arm's length, and garnered support from TV producer Norman Lear and liberal Protestants who questioned the suitability of conservative religious leaders voicing an opinion on what goes on in public life. Inasmuch as neither he nor Carter were likely to receive standing ovations at Reunion Arena in Dallas, they stayed home.

There were a good many reasons this crowd preferred Reagan. For one, he did not disdain their values, and he did not dismiss them as second-class citizens because they embraced certain rock-ribbed beliefs. He even went so far as to question the teaching of evolution in public schools. At one point many evangelicals regarded John Connally as an attractive candidate. A number of pastors met with him on his Texas ranch in the summer of 1979. During the discussion James Kennedy asked, "If you were to die tomorrow, Governor, and you wanted to go to heaven, what reason would you give God for letting you in?" Connally replied, "Well, my mother was a Methodist, my pappy was a Methodist, my grandmother was a Methodist, and I'd just tell him I ain't any worse than any of the other people that want to get into heaven."

John Conlan, who was present, said this fell like a stone on all these Christian leaders. A short time later, some of the same people met with Reagan in the Capitol Hilton Hotel in Washington. This time Memphis pastor Lane Adams asked the question. "Reagan dropped his eyes, looked at his feet and said, 'I wouldn't give God any reason for letting me in. I'd just ask for mercy, because of what Jesus Christ did for me at Calvary.'" Conlan noted, "To every man and woman in that room, they said, 'Let's go!' and they went all out for him."

James Robison and John Connally picked Reagan up at the airport. As Robison remembers, "We had a private meeting with him. I told him that since we could not endorse him as a body, it would probably be wise if his opening comment would be, 'I know this is non-partisan, so you can't endorse me, but I want you to know that I endorse you.' Oh, he loved that. He wrote that down and said, 'That's great, I'm going to use that.'"

Prior to going on stage, Ed McAteer gripped Ronald Reagan's hand, and said, "Let's pray." "Let's do it," Reagan responded, as some twenty or thirty men and women joined hands. Reagan's aides wanted the former governor to stay backstage until he was introduced, but he chose otherwise. He liked people and enjoyed the give-and-take of the audience, and being there gave him the opportunity to take the pulse of the crowd and identify with it. It was one of the secrets of the Great Communicator. In addition to that, Connally had urged him to go out and sit on the platform. "I'd like you to hear James," he said, "you're really going to like him. And it will say a lot to the people to watch how you respond to the values he's going to emphasize. Your countenance is going to do a lot."

Michael Deaver and Ed Meese weren't too happy when Reagan joined the others on the platform and was seated with

James Kennedy on one side and Dallas pastor W.A. Criswell on the other.

Reagan listened and applauded, smiled and nodded his head as Robison spoke, and the people loved it. Robison was involved in planning the session in which Reagan would speak. "I felt I could say what we were thinking as effectively as anyone could and definitely wanted the opportunity to speak just before the President. Others may have wished for the opportunity, but you have to make decisions, and I made that one." The evangelist was in great form that night. William Martin in *With God on Our Side* described him as "a big raw-boned, ruggedly handsome, compelling speaker, regarded by many as one of the very best crusade evangelists."

"I really appreciate your applause," said Robison, "because I know you're not applauding men. You are applauding the greatest country on the face of this earth and you want it to continue to be the greatest country on the face of this earth.

"I am convinced it is the greatest nation on the face of the earth because of its heritage and foundation. Proverbs 14:34 says, 'Righteousness exalts a nation but sin is a reproach to any people.'

"There is no possible way you can separate God from government and have a successful government," he continued, his speech punctuated with shouts of 'Amen.'

"When the righteous," he thundered, "when the pro-family, the moral, the biblical, the hard-working and the decent individual stays out of politics, who on earth does that leave to make the policies that affect our lives?"

It was exhortation and instruction, commendation and encouragement — and a little scolding, "How can you expect the godly to get elected if godly people don't support and vote for them? How can men who stand on principle govern if the people who stand on principle don't even vote? We're the guilty ones."

At one point, Sen. Jesse Helms leaned over and tapped

Reagan and asked, "How are you going to follow this?" "Gonna be tough," Reagan quipped, "gonna be tough."

Waving a Bible, Robison challenged the people, "You ought to read this book sometimes. This Bible has the answers and is more relevant than tomorrow morning's newspaper." Then he finished with a flourish, "We either get right with God or we're right in a position for someone to come in and take over this country. Unless we trust God, this government is finished."

The thunderous applause spoke volumes. Somebody was speaking for the people, and they would no longer be silent. It was time to take back the government. The call had gone out and they were ready to respond.

Reagan's aides were cringing and saying, "Where in the world did this guy come from?" But *New York Times* reporter Kenneth Briggs was impressed: "James Robison is one of the most powerful preachers I've ever seen. He could preach the wax off chairs. He had people in the palm of his hands."

Ronald Reagan had the pulse of this crowd and when James Kennedy introduced him, he stepped to the podium and said, "I know this is non-partisan, so you can't endorse me, but I want you to know that I endorse you."

Twenty thousand people were on their feet. "Any lingering hesitation the New Evangelical Right had about backing Ronald Reagan was swept away," said Martin.

"When I hear the First Amendment used as a reason to keep traditional moral values away from policymaking," Reagan began, "I am shocked. The First Amendment was written not to protect the people and their laws from religious values but to protect those values from government, but over the last two or three decades, the federal government seems to have forgotten both 'that old-time religion' and that old-time Constitution.

"The office of the presidency must ensure that the awesome power of government respects the rights of parents and the integrity of the family. If a President can propose taxes, regulations, controls and embargoes, he can propose, as well, ways to keep big government out of the school and the neighborhood and above all — the home."

This was the kind of straight talk these folks understood and wanted to hear. This was the kind of leadership they were ready to follow. They welcomed a reminder of who they are and where they came from and were in no mood to settle for something less.

"We can exert America's moral leadership in the world again," Reagan asserted. "And, most important, we can get back to the idea that in a struggle against totalitarian tyranny, traditional values based on religious morality are among our great strengths."

By the time Reagan concluded, there were no illusions: The ground *was* shifting that day in Texas, and the resulting reconfiguration of the political landscape would be felt for years to come.

A Gallup poll released September 7 showed Republican organizers had a long way to go. President Carter still enjoyed a big lead among evangelical Christians and he was ahead among the total of voters. But in the minds and hearts of the people who came to Texas, victory was in sight. "This movement will put Ronald Reagan in office," declared the Roundtable's founder, Southern Baptist layman Ed McAteer. And it happened. Overwhelming President Carter with more than 60 percent of the vote, on November 4, 1980, the former actor from California was elected president of the United States.

A short time later McAteer was worshiping in the First Baptist Church in Dallas when the pastor, W.A. Criswell, recognized him, and said, "I see my good friend Ed McAteer in the congregation this morning — Ed McAteer, the maker of presidents."

This is the story of that man and his movement, and the significant role they played in the realignment of political forces in this country, who believed with Ronald Reagan that "if we ordinary citizens don't run government, government is going to run us."

CHAPTER 2

HUMBLE BEGINNINGS

On August 26, we sat together in Ed McAteer's home to begin investigating the life of this interesting man. It was a beautiful day in Memphis. The sun was bright and the sky was clear. Ed, however, had a smile on his face that made the bright day outside seem dull in comparison.

As we sat in his large office, we were surrounded by scores of pictures, some autographed and others included Ed with an individual or group of famous people. The pictures on the walls encompassed a veritable "Who's Who" of American life for the last thirty years. In addition to all the photos, there were plaques and awards that dotted the walls giving recognition and honor to the man whose life-story you now hold in your hand.

One magazine cover caught my attention above all the others. It was not the biggest or the most colorful, but my eyes were drawn to it like a moth to a flame. Framed very simply, the cover read in boxcar letters, "The 100 Most Influential People in America." And there he was, pictured among one of the 100 –Ed McAteer.

Was Ed born into this influence? Was his family and

upbringing that of the cultured elite of America? Did he have a silver spoon in his mouth from childhood? My mind recalled a story I had read not long ago. An American tourist was visiting France. He came to a small but ancient town in the heartland of that country. The sign gave the name of the city and the date it was established –737 AD. An old, weathered Frenchman sat on a bench by the town square. The tourist asked, "Sir, this is an old city. Any famous people born here?" "No famous people born in this town," the old man replied, "only babies."

Ed McAteer was born to a common set of parents on July 29, 1926, in Memphis, Tennessee. At the time, Memphis was the queen city of the Mid-South with a population of approximately 212,000. The city was known for its national cotton industry, clean neighborhoods, strong work ethic, blues and jazz music, the political machine of E.H. Crump, friendly people, and the mighty Mississippi River.

Ed was born in the John Gaston Hospital. John Gaston Hospital replaced an outdated, deteriorating three-story Memphis General Hospital that had been built in 1898. The hospital was the pride and joy of the city. It had six stories and a basement, with a terraced entrance. It was called the most up-to-date and beautiful hospital in the South, with spacious wards housing 22 beds each. The wards had southern exposure windows and ceiling fans. The hospital could house 550 patients.

John Gaston Hospital was dedicated to the care of the indigent ill of Memphis and Shelby County. The city took care of the business end while the University of Tennessee handled the medical side. Patients were admitted to the hospital either through the emergency room or the outpatient clinic. More than 500 patients a day were seen in the clinics. His birth certificate read Edward Eugene McAteer. His father's family was Irish Catholic. Ed's grandfather had emigrated to America from Ireland and settled in Illinois. His mother and her family were from Tennessee. Ed was the second child born to his parents; three more siblings would follow.

Ed only has the slightest memory of his mother, for she

died when he was four years old. One would think, therefore, that Ed, his brother and three sisters were all raised by their father. Such was not the case and here's why. Ed's father was a Merchant Marine. He literally traveled all over the world in his job. Ed recalls, "I can only remember seeing my father twice in my whole life. Those two times he just came for a brief visit and left again. He was not with me as I grew up."

Letters from his father did arrive in the mailbox where Ed lived. The letters came from England, France, Spain, Italy, and other parts of the world. In 1939, when Ed was almost thirteen years old, he was told his father had died. "What was my father like? Why did he leave us? Was he cold-hearted?" Ed would ask those questions for many years. He never knew the answer until Ed and his wife, Faye, celebrated their fiftieth wedding anniversary in 1998. As an anniversary gift, a friend researched Ed's genealogy. They uncovered much information about Ed's father. He was not a hard-hearted man. Ed told us, "My father was a very distraught man. America was in the early years of the Great Depression when my mother died. My father was bothered by the fear that he could not supply needed money for his family. One out of four working Americans were out of work. He accepted a dependable job with the Merchant Marines and that took him away from us. He did not come home. I hold no grudges."

Ed and his siblings were now officially orphans. What happened to them? His mother's family was compassionate and stepped in to help. The five children were split up among relatives, Ed being taken by his mother's sister in Memphis. "Although technically an orphan, I never felt like one. My aunt and uncle treated me with great love," Ed says today.

His uncle and aunt, Henry and Viola May, were not wealthy people. As a matter of fact, the record shows they were quite poor. Like millions of other people during the Depression, family needs were met on a week-to-week basis; sometimes it was day-to-day. Smiling, Ed told us, "As I grew up with my aunt and uncle, we were poor in money, but we were rich in character. I sure didn't know what wall-to-wall carpet was, but I did know what wall-to-wall love was all about."

Henry and Viola May were people of strong character. They were devout people who personally had a private devotion to God. In their home, however, there was no talk of religion. Ed's elementary years in this house were happy years. Ed laughed often and easily. He never remembers being mistreated or ignored, but he received very little direction and self-discipline for future life.

Ed had a quick mind and a strong body as a boy growing up in South Memphis. He was given a second-hand bike that he rode all over his neighborhood. Like any boy, the faster he could ride, the better he liked it. Ed also loved to swim. Memphis weather in the summer was always hot and humid. Of course, air conditioning was unknown. Ponds and rivers were favorite hangouts for Ed and his friends during the sizzling days of summer. Another sport –football—also caught Ed's attention and time, but it was baseball that really captured Ed's heart.

During the late 1930s in America, baseball truly was America's pastime. Household names like Joe DiMaggio, Lou Gehrig, Bob Feller, and a rising star by the name of Ted Williams grabbed headlines across America making many boys in our nation dream of playing in the big leagues. Ed was one of those boys and his dreams were big.

Ed recalls, "Sometime during 1937 we got our first radio. One thing I listened to whenever I was able was baseball games." What an era for baseball it was. New York had three teams; the Yankees, the Giants, and the Dodgers. The Boston Red Sox were rivals to all the New York teams, and then when you add the St. Louis Cardinals and their Gashouse Gang, the Detroit Tigers and the Philadelphia Athletics, baseball had all the making of pure magic for the boy Ed McAteer growing up in Memphis.

In ninth grade, Ed was the starting pitcher for his school team. He had a fastball that he thought rivaled Dizzy Dean's.

"I always played hard and wanted to win, but I always played fair." Then the Chevrolet dealers in Memphis decided to sponsor a boy's baseball team. Ed tried out and made the team as a pitcher. This allowed him to play teams across Memphis and also to travel a little in the Mid-South playing ball. The Memphis Chevrolet team was good and won the league championship one year. It was perhaps the first trophy Ed was awarded, but it would not be the last award for accomplishments in his unfolding life.

What about Ed and his school life? "I was not a brilliant student," Ed often says with a twinkle in his eye, "but neither did I flunk out. I worked hard and I guess you can just call me average." Being a healthy child, Ed rarely missed school. He made friends easily and had much fun during his years in school.

It is always interesting to see how a person forms habits, interests, and hobbies in their formative years that stay with them throughout their life. For Ed, his favorite subjects in school were reading, English, basic arithmetic, and history. As a boy of twelve, he was fascinated by the stories of King Arthur and his knights at the roundtable. Ed would read the adventures of King Arthur and see the pictures in the books, and his mind would be flooded with vivid imaginations. "Remember," Ed mused, "this happened to me during the lean years of the Depression. Jobs were tough to find and did not pay much money. Often the meals we ate were sufficient, but rarely was there abundance. To see pictures of tables full and overflowing with food stuck like glue in my mind when I was a boy. I could only imagine what it must have been like to have and eat that much food!"

Looking back with hindsight, it's interesting to realize that Ed's mind was captured by the adventures of King Arthur and his knights when he was a boy. Like those men of adventure, bravery, and love for their country, Ed would grow into manhood and experience his own degree of adventure, bravery, and love for his country and God in all the efforts he would take on. Let the reader also connect the fact that as a boy, Ed read voraciously about King Arthur and his roundtable. One must ask what influence that had on the boy McAteer when he would later found his own Roundtable that would make its mark on the political and religious scene in America during the last two decades of the twentieth century.

As we talked that August day about his childhood, Ed leaned back in his chair, put his right hand up to his chin, and added, "Some of the things we are talking about I haven't thought about for years, but other experiences from my childhood I reflect on often." Ed then began to nod his head. With eyes as clear as crystal, his voice dropped a notch as he told us, "About age twelve, maybe it was when I was thirteen, but right at that time, I was drawn to Christian American history. I read and read and read everything I could get my hands on that talked about our Founding Fathers' and later leaders' commitment to and discussions about God's sovereignty over America." Then Ed began to tell us about George Washington in his inaugural address in 1789 when he stated, "The propitious smiles of heaven can never be expected on a nation that disregards the eternal rules of order and right which heaven itself has ordained." From there he moved to Benjamin Franklin, not viewed by most as an overtly Christian man, but nonetheless a man with a strong biblical and Christian foundation from his childhood. During the wrangling of the Constitutional Convention in 1787, Franklin stood and addressed the chairman: "I therefore beg leave to move that henceforth, prayers imploring the assistance of heaven and its blessing upon our deliberations be held every morning in this assembly. Without God's help, we shall accomplish nothing more than to build another Tower of Babel."

Ed was on a roll and his memory was brilliant. He spoke of Thomas Jefferson and his Notes on the State of Virginia in 1781: "I tremble for my country when I reflect that God is just and that His justice cannot sleep forever." As Ed spoke, anyone could hear and feel the settled conviction in his voice. He jumped ahead in our nation's history to 1863 and Abraham Lincoln's proclamation of a national day of prayer and fasting: "It behooves us then to humble ourselves before the offended Power, to confess our national sins, and pray for clemency and forgiveness."

To this day, Ed McAteer and his wife read a paragraph or two every morning after breakfast on the subject of Christian American history. The authors were all impressed by Ed's ability to recall and quote poems, phrases, and sections of speeches. As Ed spoke, his entire demeanor changed. As we sat listening, it was like hearing one of our original Founding Fathers speak to us from the deepest conviction of his heart. You see, Ed McAteer not only knows the words of history, but is convinced those words still apply to out nation today.

Before we moved on to ask about his earliest jobs, Ed bounced up in his chair to the very edge (we thought he might fall out of the chair!) and excitedly said, "Oh, there's one more and it's one of my favorites. It's those famous words from the Frenchman Alexis de Tocqueville.

"I sought for the key to the greatness and genius of America in her harbors; in her fertile fields and boundless forests; in her rich mines and vast world commerce; in her public school system and institutions of learning. I sought for it in her democratic Congress and in her matchless constitution.

"Not until I went into the churches of America and heard her pulpits aflame with righteousness did I understand the secret of her genius and power.

"America is great because America is good, and if America ever ceases to be good, America will cease to be great."

Ed's boyhood interest in Christian American history has never waned. It is still inspiring, guiding, and calling him to this day.

In 1937, the house where Ed was living purchased its first radio. In those days, radio was still young. At times, the reception would be poor and there would be some crackling during the programs. Of course, digital tuning was still off in the future, so the old analog tuning was the best technology of the day. But Ed and the rest of the household were amazed.

What did the family listen to in 1937? The choices were not broad, but Ed recalls listening to mystery theaters, baseball games, and boxing matches. The vivid imagination of a boy like Ed could paint pictures in his mind as he heard the voice over the radio tell the mystery story or give a play-by-play description of the sporting event.

"I also remember President Roosevelt delivering his fireside chats," Ed reminisces. "We would sit by the radio in our house in Memphis and listen to our President talk to us about the world, the nation, the economy, and life. It was so amazing! As a boy I felt like I was sitting right next to the President of the United States of America and he was talking to me. If I closed my eyes, it was like I could have reached out and touched him" Little did that boy in Memphis know that one day he would sit next to Presidents and literally be able to reach over and touch them, as well as influence their policy in America and overseas.

School would always break for vacation during the hot, humid months of June, July and August in Memphis. When Ed was just a small boy, summer vacation from school was spent playing outdoors with his friends. The summer that Ed turned ten, he began to work to earn some money. "A fine Italian family with the last name of Ventrini grew vegetables in a hothouse on the south side of Memphis. It was very near to where the International Airport is located today," Ed recalls. "They grew tomatoes, okra, turnips, green beans – a real variety of vegetables. Mr. Ventrini would sell his produce to the stores in Memphis, and also take baskets downtown and sell at the farmer's market."

At age ten, Ed's job was to weed the lines of vegetables, and then pick them when they were ripe. "It was hard, hot work. When you're that age and it's your first job, you want to do your best. I'd work until my back ached and my hands hurt." The highlight of the day was lunch. Ed would eat the bag lunch his aunt would pack him and he felt like a real man. Ed was paid fifty cents a day for his work. He recalls fondly that he was proud to have a job. After all, the Depression still had an ugly grip on America. It also taught Ed the value of an honest day's work.

When Ed turned thirteen years old and summer vacation from school came, he had his eye on another job. He was physically strong for his age, so he landed a summer job working on a digger's pole. He was responsible to operate a machine that would drill through gravel and down into the sub-soil to test its compaction. There's no question that it was a man's job, but Ed was up to the work both physically and mentally. "Remember," Ed smiled, "this was summer in Memphis, Tennessee. The temperature would soar to 95°, the humidity would almost match that number, and the sun was a bronze ball of fire in the sky shooting its piercing rays at us all day long." It was extremely hard work done over very long days. Ed was paid $1 per day for this job, doubling what he was paid at his earlier job. "Was that job tough?" Ed asked himself. "Without question. Was it worth it? Absolutely, for it allowed me at a young age to spread my wings and experience what hard work and long days were all about." The job at the digger's pole left an impression on the young McAteer that is still with him today. Be unafraid to work hard and do your best at everything.

High school days for Ed seemed to fly by so swiftly. America had entered World War II in 1941 as Ed was beginning his days in high school. Many of his older friends were going off to war immediately after their graduation. It was no different for Ed. In the spring of 1943, he promptly joined the war effort and it was off to fight in the South Pacific. The boy with humble beginnings was taking his first steps toward patriotism and valor.

CHAPTER 3

A COMPASS FOR LIFE

A day in the life of Ed McAteer is never dull or slow. As we arrived at Ed's home for this interview one Tuesday, the phones were ringing and the fax machines were going off constantly. An efficient office staff was stuffing editorials written by Ed that would be mailed to over six hundred major papers across the nation. McAteer was at it again, working to get his well-thought out convictions to the media so Americans could hear another voice of reason.

Who is this man? What drives him? You see, everybody is driven by something. Webster defines the verb "drive" as "to guide, to control, or to direct." Whether a person is driving a car, a nail, or a golf ball, you are working to guide it at that moment. What drives Ed McAteer? What is his internal compass?

Anyone who meets Ed will quickly discover that three things drive him. One, his devotion to God — it's clear and evident. Two, his love for his wife and family – that is heard and felt. Last, his loyalty to his country — that is significant and unchanging. Let's move inside Ed McAteer. Let us attempt to uncover what makes him "tick." Our goal is to put our finger on his internal compass.

Henry and Viola May, the uncle and aunt who raised McAteer, had a private and quiet devotion to God. Ed recalls, "My uncle and aunt were good people, very good people. They worked hard, provided for me, and loved me, but they did not talk much, if ever, about their belief in and devotion to God Almighty." As a boy growing up, Ed had very few thoughts about God or visits to church during the first fifteen years of his life.

At age fifteen, a friend invited Ed to go to church with him. "It was a Methodist church in Oakville, Tennessee, not too far from my house in Memphis." McAteer recalls that it was an old-fashioned Methodist church. That congregation was having revival meetings at the time. Ed was a teenager and remembers, "The people were so friendly. The singing was spirited and joyful. The sermon the pastor preached that night had my name all over it." As the man spoke in church from behind the pulpit, Ed listened to every word. The young McAteer liked what he heard. It made total sense to him. At the end of the preacher's sermon, he invited everyone who wanted to become a Christian and follow the Lord Jesus for his or her whole life to "stand up, walk down that aisle, kneel at this altar, and repent of your sin." Ed was one of the first one who stood up and walked forward. That day at age fifteen, Ed prayed to confess Jesus Christ as his Savior.

"We didn't stay inside the church too long after the meeting ended, but we sure stayed long enough for God to change my life," Ed said with a smile. "When I walked outside that night, the air seemed fresher, the stars shone brighter, and I felt as if Someone was walking right next to me." When Ed awakened the next day, the sense and reality of the Lord's work in him was still evident. This young man knew he had experienced something real. Ed McAteer had become a Christian. His life was changed forever.

This experience Ed had with God took place as he was about to enter high school. "During my middle teen years in high school," Ed reports, "I stumbled along in my Christian life. I rarely prayed or read the Bible. The same was true during my days in the Navy. To be honest, my spiritual life during the war years even dipped below that of high school. I saw no growth in the Lord or any witness for Christ coming from my life." Spiritually, Ed's life was on a flat-line.

After Ed was discharged from the Navy, he returned to Memphis. Enthusiasm in America was running sky high. A bloody and costly war was over. Servicemen were everywhere on the streets of America and they were honored as heroes. Organizations were emerging to serve the physical, financial, educational, and spiritual needs of the boys returning from the war. In the latter category, Youth for Christ was one such organization. Dr. Bob Cook and Torrey Johnson began this ministry in Chicago, but it soon outgrew the windy city. Youth for Christ had young, energetic speakers that held meetings across America to ask young people to give their lives to Christ. (Billy Graham was one of the young evangelists Youth for Christ used in 1946-47. This was before Billy Graham received national recognition from his August 1949 tent meetings in Los Angeles where Randolph Hearst gave Graham huge headlines in his papers.)

In 1946, Youth for Christ rented the Ellis Auditorium in downtown Memphis. "The place was packed out," Ed told us. "There were young people my age everywhere. I had never experienced anything like it. It was so different from a church service as I knew it." That was the goal of Youth for Christ. Their slogan at that time was "Geared to the times, but anchored to the Rock." In other words, this organization aimed at being contemporary and relevant to the youth culture in the late 1940s, but at the same time true and faithful to the beliefs of historic Christianity.

As the boxing champ and war hero sat in the Ellis Auditorium that night, memory took him by the hand and led him back to that Methodist church meeting when he was fifteen. "I experienced the same thing in Ellis Auditorium that night as I did at that Methodist church. The people were so friendly and really cared about me. The music was great and the message from the speaker was clear and relevant." (To this day, Ed cannot remember who the speaker was, but it does not matter for God had an appointment with Ed McAteer that night.) As the meeting came to a conclusion, all those who desired to dedicate their lives to Jesus Christ were invited to walk to the front of the auditorium. Hundreds of young people walked forward that night, and among the many was Ed. "I was already a Christian, but my spiritual life was flat, blah, and going nowhere fast," Ed asserted. "I walked to the front of Ellis Auditorium to rededicate my life to Christ."

Emmett Maum was in the crowd that night and served as a counselor with Youth for Christ. Mr. Maum was a member of Memphis First Assembly of God, one of the leading churches in the city, and a sports writer for the Commercial Appeal, the leading paper in Memphis. Maum had covered Ed as a boxer in previous months. He spotted Ed in the crowd of those who came forward that night. Maum weaved his way through the crowd until he was standing next to Ed.

"Emmett was a wonderful Christian man. He prayed with me that night and gave me so much encouragement. What a help he was to me as a young Christian," Ed recalls. "I also think he gave me a little more press in his writing about boxing as a sports editor. He liked me and I admired him. Emmett Maum was a great help to both my spiritual and my boxing career."

Most people have someone who is the major influence in their life. Who was it that most influenced Ed McAteer in his spiritual life? The answer to that question is Faye Carter, the young lady who would soon become Ed's wife. Faye is the opposite of Ed in many ways. While Ed is out-going, she is more retiring. If Ed walked into a crowded auditorium, he would seek for a seat in the front row; Faye would glance at the back row. Whereas Ed was raised by a loving couple who rarely spoke about Christ or visited church, Faye's home was 180 degrees opposite of that lifestyle. Yet God used tall, elegant, charming young Faye Carter to stir Ed and put within him a desire to know and serve God.

Faye Carter was born to godly parents in Crocket County, Tennessee. (It was from this county that Davy Crocket went to fight in the Texas Alamo, and hence the name Crocket County.) Faye's heritage on both her father's and mother's side was devout, practicing Christians. "My mother began taking me to church when I was two weeks old," Faye told me. "Of course I don't remember that, but I do remember there was never a time we did not go to church."

Faye's father was a well-known and prosperous farmer in Crocket County. He was the chairman of the board of deacons in their local church and also one of the teachers in the church. Ed said of him, "Her daddy was one of the finest Christian men I've ever met in my travels all over the world." Mr. Carter was a big man. Ed reported to us that Faye's daddy had such a big hand that one of his little fingers would cover up both of Ed's thumbs. "Mr. Harles Carter was a gentle giant," Ed smiled as he reflected back. "He could take a Coke top off a bottle – the ones you had to pry off with a bottle opener – and crush it between his thumb and index finger." Ed had a good friend by the name of Fred Minton. He played baseball at the University of Oklahoma, and then was signed by the old Brooklyn Dodgers. While visiting the McAteers one day, they took him to meet Mr. Carter. After Minton met him and shook his hand, he stated, "There's only one other man I've ever met in all my life who had such a big hand, and that was Gil Hodges." Mr. Carter not only had a big hand, but he also had a big heart. Crocket County used to give out an award for the outstanding family of the year. For the year of 1939, the Carter family was honored with this award.

Growing up as a girl, Faye enjoyed basketball, piano, and reading. She graduated from Alamo High School in 1942 and immediately enrolled at Memphis State University. There she distinguished herself as a student and a leader. Faye completed a double major in English and chemistry, completing this four-year degree in three years. While at the university, she was the vice president of her sorority, crowned the May Princess, graduated with honors, and was named to Who's Who Among American College Students. All through her high school and college life, Faye was a growing, dynamic Christian whose life was a clear witness and example of Jesus Christ.

How did Ed and Faye first meet? Well, they agree completely on the facts of that first meeting, but their perceptions are very different. When Faye graduated from Memphis State she took a job in early 1946 as a lab technician at Kennedy Hospital in Memphis. Ed was also in Memphis at that time attending Southern Law School. "The G.I Bill was paying my school tuition," Ed told us, "but I needed some extra spending money. I had heard that Kennedy Hospital would pay $10 per unit to people with my blood type, so I decided to go and donate blood." The day Ed went to give blood, Faye was assigned to draw the blood. "When Ed came in," Faye told me, "I had never met him before, and as I drew his blood, he was ever so friendly with me. At first I thought he was too friendly." Ed liked what he saw in this young girl. He turned on his charm and began to tease and flirt. To this day, Ed maintains Faye liked him from first sight and brought him six or seven glasses of orange juice after she drew his blood. "Oh no," responds Faye, "one glass of juice was the policy, and one glass he got. I saw Ed as just another arm from which to draw blood!" Little did Faye realize that this arm would one day be around her and hold her in marriage for well over fifty years.

What's the truth about that first meeting? It's most likely a combination of the two stories, but the outcome was a date between Ed and Faye was set. "Our very first date was when we went to see the movie 'O.S.S.' starring Alan Ladd," Faye said with a smile. "I forget where we went to eat, but I enjoyed my time with Ed." When Ed asked Faye out the second time, she accepted, but requested that she would like Ed to come to church with her. "Go to church!" Ed protested with an inflected voice. "I sure wasn't a heathen, but neither did I spend my time going to church. This was all new to me, but I liked this girl, so I agreed to go." Ed was a Christian at this point, but Jesus was not Lord of his life. "I think I had a spiritual mind," Ed said, "but not a faithful, spiritual life. For example, I can only recall one time in my life when I used the Lord's name in vain. I was in the Navy on board the St. Lo. I blurted out a curse word. I felt so bad. My action cut me deep in my heart." But God had now put Faye in Ed's life. She would not only win his heart, but the Lord would use Faye to point Ed's heart to God. He was beginning to know what it meant, "to seek first the kingdom of God and His righteousness" (Matthew 6:33).

Ed grew fond of Faye very quickly, but he realized he had competition. "You see," Ed whispered as his eyes widened, "when I began to date Faye, she was also dating three other young men. They were all fine young men. That's the only kind Faye would date. I knew I just had to outsell myself over those other three." Ed and Faye began to date more frequently. Her relationship with the other three grew less and less. After two years, Ed was ready to ask this young lady from Crocket County to be his wife. "Faye, did Ed surprise you with the ring?" we asked. "Oh no, there are no surprises with Ed McAteer. He gets all excited over even the smallest things. No, I can read him like a book," Faye replied lovingly. When she drove home from Memphis to tell her mother about the wedding, Mrs. Carter said, "My little girl is engaged! How exciting! Who is it – Jack or Johnny?" (These were two other boys Faye had dated.) "Oh no, Momma, it's Eddie – Eddie McAteer!"

On December 19, 1948, Ed and Faye were married at Johnson Grove Baptist church. This was a small church, so the wedding was the event of the season. Faye wore a gold colored bridal gown. "She was radiant that day," Ed told us, "absolutely radiant!" Faye did not like big, splashy events, so she chose only one bridesmaid to be in her wedding. The ceremony was simple, but it was beautiful. Because Faye's family was so well known in the church and around the area, there was an overflow crowd for the wedding. People were seated and standing in every spare spot.

In the earliest days of their marriage, Ed realized that his new wife was every inch a classy lady. She had poise, dignity, grace, and beauty. Faye soon understood she had a husband who was an eternal optimist and possessed a wonderful sense of humor. Ed has always loved to pull pranks and enjoys a good laugh. All his friends know that at times Ed will call and disguise his voice. He will pretend he is someone else, playing with and confusing the one he has called. Then he will laugh and say, "This is really your old friend Ed McAteer." One of the authors remembers a time that Ed was going into a store. The nine-time Grammy winner, nationally famous singer James Blackwood was coming out of the store. (When James was home and off the road from his singing for a week, he would totally unwind. He would not shave for two or three days at a time and wear old, tattered jeans around town.) The two friends stopped outside the store to talk. As they ended, Ed put his hand on James' shoulder and prayed for him. It was winter and Blackwood was wearing an old coat with a stocking cap pulled down on his head. Someone saw Ed praying for this man and later told him, "Ed, it's so wonderful how you care for all people. I saw you praying for that old, dirty, homeless man outside Walgreen's yesterday. I'm proud of you." Ed never told them it was the legendary James Blackwood, but Ed did tell James the story and they laughed loud and long together. Ed does have a sense of humor.

Faye watched her new husband grow spiritually. "Ed is a fair, loving husband," Faye says. "He's a good father and carries his load. He has clear convictions. Through our years of marriage, he maintains his personal time of Bible reading and prayer. I have often found Ed up at 4 a.m. reading his Bible, praying for his family, and asking God to bless our nation." Like everyone, Ed McAteer does have an internal compass. It deviated during the early years of his life, but the Lord used

Faye as the human instrument to direct the compass in Ed's heart. Now, there is no question where that compass points: to God, to morality, to family, to life and freedom.

CHAPTER 4

BOXING CHAMP AND WAR HERO

A red-letter date in the history books of the United States of America is December 7, 1941. The color red not only marked its importance in national and world history, but it was additionally the day that hundreds of U.S. servicemen shed their bright red blood as America was plunged into World War II with the Japanese attack on Pearl Harbor.

President Franklin Roosevelt spoke to Congress and the nation the next day. FDR referred to December 7 as "a day that would live in infamy." For over two years since Nazi Germany invaded Poland in September of 1939 and World War II began, America had officially stayed out of the massive conflict. Now everything changed with the attack on Pearl Harbor. There was no option, no question; America declared war against Japan, Germany, and Italy.

Patriotism surged throughout our nation and coursed through the veins of young men. FDR continued to galvanize the nation with his radio addresses while newspapers printed pictures and details of fierce battles. The sight of young men in uniform stirred the emotions of citizens all across the country.

Ed McAteer was nearly sixteen yeas old when the attack

on Pearl Harbor occurred. "Of course I remember that day. Who could ever forget it? The thoughts, the words, the emotions are still vivid in my mind. I could take you to the spot I was standing when I heard the news," Ed stated. The readiness to enlist and the rising patriotism found a willing heart in the young sixteen-year-old.

Ed began to think, "What will be my part? Will I see combat? Will I come back home alive? What will be the outcome of this war in the world?" From childhood Ed had read the adventures of King Arthur and his knights of the roundtable. That was all boyhood fascination, but this was real war. Everyday young soldiers were giving their lives for their country.

Ed also had a deep sense of patriotism. For five or six years, he had immersed himself in reading the stirring stories and speeches of our Founding Fathers. Ed knew of their dedication to freedom and protection of our country. He knew that he too would enlist to fight for America and help keep her a free nation. But what branch of service would be his choice? The Army? The Marines? Air Force? The Navy? Although Ed only saw his father twice in his life, he knew the man was in the Merchant Marines and sailed the world. Ed made his choice. He would serve his nation and his president as a sailor in the United States Navy.

Ed left Whitehaven High School in Memphis in June of 1943. Like so many of his buddies, there was little discussion what their future would be for the next few years. A war had to be won. In the spring of 1943, Ed enlisted in the U.S. Navy and was sent to the San Diego Naval Base for training.

In the summer of 1943, America was neck-deep in World War II. Forty percent of the gross domestic product was being poured into the war effort. Ships needed to be built, planes constructed, ammunition supplied, and service men and women supported. Massive amounts of money were being spent. The naval base in San Diego was just one example. "It was huge and busy," Ed recalls. "I recall my first week in training. I had never seen anything like it before in my life."

Fighting men were needed on both the European and Pacific fronts. Twelve weeks of rigorous training were given to the recruits. "Of course the training was tough, long, intense, and required a great deal of discipline," Ed said matter-of-factly, "but after all, we were at war. We were facing life and death issues as a nation and as sailors. We were all well aware that some of us in training would not come back home. It wasn't a morbid thought, but it was a fact of life."

Ed found little time to relax during his intense twelve weeks of training in San Diego. When he did have a little free time, young McAteer got involved heavily in the Navy's boxing program. Boxing was nothing new to him by this time in his life. Let's take a brief look back into Ed's life before we sail off to war and experience the greatest sea battle ever fought.

When Ed was only ten years old, his grandfather on his mother's side was a big boxing fan. "Jack Dempsey was my grandfather's hero. He felt there was no one better with his hands in the ring than Dempsey." Ed would listen to his grandfather talk of boxing. He watched the old man. At times they would playfully jab each other back and forth. "When we got the first radio in our house, I would tune in the fights," Ed said with a smile. The signal on the radio was not always clear and static was common, but the boy McAteer had a vivid imagination. As the announcer would give a blow-by-blow account of the fight, to Ed it was as if the contest was being fought in his kitchen! At times he would jump to his feet, get in a boxing stance, and dance around the room, jabbing at an imaginary opponent. "Of course, I always won all those imaginary fights. I was undefeated in every fight in which I boxed in my kitchen," Ed mused.

Now remember, Ed's interest in boxing began during the Depression. Money was tight and handled frugally. Boxing gloves were expensive in the Sears catalog and considered a luxury. There was no way his family could or would buy a pair of gloves for a boy. Perish the thought! "Only rich people like the Rockerfellers can afford boxing gloves," Ed thought. (And

John Rockerfeller, Sr. was rich, even during the Depression. When he died in 1937, his businesses accounted for one of every thirty dollars generated in the entire United States economy!) Since Ed could not afford to buy a pair of boxing gloves, he made his own pair. "I got an old gunny sack. I cut it up into long strips. Then I found some old rags. I put the rags around my hands, wrapped the strips of gunny cloth over the rags, and presto, I had boxing gloves!" Ed exclaimed. He would tie those homemade gloves on and shadowbox, spar with other boys his age in friendly matches, and even practice on bags filled with rags hanging from the rafters.

Ed was quick, strong, and tough. Boxing came easy and he liked it. Not only did he like it, he was also good at it. Ed could not only give a quick jab with his left hand and then a powerful shot with his big, right fist, but he also had a strong chin that could take a punch and leave him standing. That combination is important for a good boxer.

During high school, Ed joined the Golden Gloves. He would often go to the gym at the John Gaston Community Center. "I was born in the John Gaston Hospital," Ed says, "so I figured I would develop my boxing skills in the John Gaston Community Center." While there were a lot of "canvas backs" in Golden Gloves, Ed was not one of them. He easily won his first four matches. His reputation as a boxer was beginning to grow. During one fight, Ed broke his thumb. "Man, did that hurt! I did win the fight, but it was tough." A doctor put a cast on the thumb and Ed was out of action for a few weeks. Those weeks gave other boxers a chance to win a few fights.

While boxing during his Navy training in San Diego, Ed met Hubert Gray. Gray was the amateur boxing champion of Texas. They developed a brief friendship, but then shipped out from San Diego in different directions. Ed boxed often during his time in the Navy, both while at base and while on board ship. Again, we'll be back to Ed's experience on the deck of an aircraft carrier being hit and sunk by a Japanese Kamikaze pilot, but first we must jump ahead to 1945 and see Ed's conclusion to boxing.

Ed McAteer returned to Memphis in late 1945. He would go to the YMCA and box in matches. He soon gained a reputation and was named the Outstanding Boxer of the Mid-South. On January 12, 1947, Ed fought a major bout at a sold out event in Memphis. Emmett Maum, sports writer for the Commercial Appeal (the city's major newspaper), wrote these words:

"After decisions were rendered in the first six championship bouts of North Memphis Golden Gloves last night before 1,190 paid customers at Wells Community Center, a flurry of knockouts and TKOs kept the fans in a frenzy. But the finale of the night proved quite suitable for the featured spot, as Eddie McAteer and Bevo Covington, open middleweights, waged a great battle. McAteer, who had beaten Frank Smith in a thriller Friday night to reach the title round, was awarded the verdict over Covington, and mainly on the strength of a punch-filled third round. McAteer and Covington each threw rapier-like lefts that hurt, and they cut loose with an avalanche of two-fisted battling that continued until the end of the fight. They sent the spectators home with a satisfied feeling indeed." Ed went on to box in the nationals for Golden Gloves.

One day Ed was at the Memphis YMCA. A man with the ring name of "The Pittsburgh Profile" – Fritzey Ziric - was in the gym. He was the welterweight champion of the world. His nose had been broken several times and scars marked both of his cheeks. (That's why he carried the ring name "The Pittsburgh Profile.") Ed knew the Profile had recently fought Henry Armstrong (better know as Hammerin' Henry) in a highly publicized bout. Ed recalls, "At the time, Hammerin' Henry held three national titles all at the same time. However, when he fought the Pittsburgh Profile, Hammerin' Henry lost to him. So when I saw Profile in the gym one day in Memphis, I introduced myself and then I asked him, 'Hey Fritzy, how good was Armstrong?' He never stopped jabbing at the bag in front of him, and said, 'I'll tell you this much, he'll keep the flies off of you.'"

A boxing promoter, Jack Lasseroff, spotted Ed in late 1946. Mr. Lasseroff liked what he saw in the young boxer – potential and talent. Discussions and contract negotiations followed. Ed signed a contract to box professionally, but events turned and his professional boxing career never materialized. As Ed spoke, I looked around the room in his house in which we sat and I saw many boxing trophies. His boxing days taught him that in life you must have both a good offense and defense. Ed would use both in his future years helping to build Colgate Palmolive and serving by the side of national leaders. Boxing also allowed Ed to meet some famous people, like world heavyweight champ and legend Mohammed Ali.

"I was invited to Ali's home," Ed told me. "Our conversation focused on our nation and on God. As I came into his house, I said to him, 'Hey Champ, do you know I used to box years ago?' Ali looked at me. 'Show me your stuff.' He put up his hands, as if they were two targets. I jumped to a boxing stance and promptly jabbed at and hit each of his hands. The Champ smiled, 'Wow, I'm impressed! People look at you and only see a little blue-eyed man talking about God and country, and then you hit them with the old one-two.'" Boxing taught Ed many valuable lessons about life. He gave up boxing when he was twenty-one, for other more important matters were reaching for him as we shall soon see. But for now, we must rewind to 1943 and the growing war.

THE REAL FIGHT

Boxing was a diversion during Ed's Navy days, but the war in the Pacific to which Ed would head was very real. When Ed finished his basic training in San Diego, he was shipped out to the State of Washington. There he was assigned to the USS Midway, an escort carrier commissioned on October 23, 1943, and boasted a crew of about a thousand men. Sailor, Ed

McAteer, was a Third Class Petty Officer. Among his duties on board ship were to load the 40mm guns, pack parachutes, and do minor repairs on both the ship and its planes.

What was life like on board ship as the Midway steamed from the coast of Washington to the front lines of the war in the South Pacific? Ed answered, "We would take duty and rotate on two-hour watches. Remember, there was nothing but the big, blue Pacific Ocean as far as you could see in every direction." Ed recalls swabbing the decks, putting up hoses, loading guns, readying the torpedoes, and playing a few pranks on some of his buddies. "After all, I had just turned seventeen years old. This was an adventure. Growing up in Memphis I had never seen the ocean. Here I was on a massive ship sailing across the ocean and heading for battle." Ed's mind must have retraced to his times of reading about King Arthur and his roundtable. There is one major difference – the adventures of King Arthur were imaginary. The ship McAteer was on would shortly be involved in the reality of war.

The USS Midway was commissioned by the Navy with that name; however, early in October, 1944, the name of the ship was changed to the St. Lo. Where did this new name come from? Aircraft carriers were often named after famous battles. St. Lo is a town in France where a famous battle had been fought and someone in the Navy Department pushed for a name change. When Ed and the men on board the ship heard of its name change, there was an uneasy feeling. "There's an old fable among sailors," Ed told us. "It's bad luck to change the name of your ship. The fable says it spells trouble for both ship and crew." Just a fable? Of course, but this time it proved true, for within two weeks of the name change, the St. Lo would be resting on the bottom of the Pacific Ocean. Ed McAteer was about to see, feel, hear, and live through the world's largest sea battle, the Battle of Leyte Gulf.

By October of 1944, the war effort for America on both fronts was bloody, but the tide was changing in favor of the

Allies. In the European theater, D-Day had taken place four months earlier. Our soldiers on the ground were beginning to push toward Berlin. In the Pacific war with Japan, the Battle of Midway Islands was history and America won that battle. Most historians call that the early turning point of the war. Japan was getting desperate.

On October 19, 1944, Vice Admiral Takijiro Onishi, commander of Japan's First Air Fleet, announced a shocking plan during a staff meeting on Luzon. "As you know the war situation is grave," he said. "There is only one way of assuring that our meager strength will be effective to a maximum degree. That is to organize suicide attack units composed of Zero fighters armed with 550-pound bombs, with each plane to crash-dive into an enemy carrier."

The admiral made his proposal knowing that single suicide planes often did more damage than a whole squadron flown by men intent on surviving to fight again. Earlier, several pilots had impulsively crash-dived into enemy ships with devastating effect. What shocked the admiral's officers was the idea of making such attacks an official operation.

Nevertheless, a suicide air corps was formed that night. It was named Kamikaze, or Divine Wind, after the legendary typhoon that saved Japan from a 13th century Mongol invasion. The plan quickly attracted an excess of volunteers – two or three times more men than planes available. Some men showed their eagerness to join by writing their applications in blood. As a rule, expert fliers were rejected since they were needed as teachers and escort pilots; generally, the volunteers were inexperienced youths.

What the Kamikazes lacked in training, they made up for in fervor. Some were inspired by Japanese religious and military traditions of self-sacrifice. "How I appreciate this chance to die like a man!" one such pilot wrote. Others, resigned to being killed in combat anyway, welcomed the opportunity to die magnificently by sinking an important ship.

The Battle of Leyte Gulf began the morning of October

25, 1944. Ed's fleet was under the direct command of Rear Admiral Thomas Sprague. The night before combat, all men on board the St. Lo were brought in by groups for a briefing about the next day's battle. Ed recalls, "The briefing was very realistic. They didn't sugarcoat a thing as they talked to us. We were told tomorrow would be a big day. They showed us pictures of the enemy and their power. We were informed how many Japanese planes and ships would most likely be involved in the attack. Our commanding officers told us of the possibility of our death and even presented a number of how many casualties they anticipated on our side. It was all very sobering." Ed and all the men on the St. Lo had a restless night of sleep on October 24, 1944.

As Ed filed out of the briefing room that night with the other men, he heard these words on the loudspeaker system of the ship: "And now live from the Grand Ole Opry in Nashville, Tennessee, it's Roy Acuff." As Ed listened, he thought of his home and family in Memphis (only 200 miles west of the Grand Ole Opry). His mind filled with memories and his bloodstream charged with adrenalin. Then Roy Acuff began to sing, *Low and lonely, sad and blue, thinking only of little you; always trying to keep from crying; I'm low and lonely over you.* Ed said tears filled his eyes. "Here I was, a boy from Tennessee listening to Roy Acuff sing from Nashville while I'm half way around the world waiting to fight in a battle that just might mean the end of my life." Years later Ed told that story to Roy Acuff. At the time, Ed was running for the U.S. Senate against Al Gore. McAteer was in Nashville at Opryland for a fundraiser. Acuff was at the same meeting, for he was running for governor of Tennessee at the time. When Ed saw him, he slapped Acuff on the back and said, "Let me tell you a true story that happened many years ago and involves you." As Roy heard the story, it moved him just as it moved Ed that night as he walked on the flight deck of the St. Lo in Leyte.

THE DAY THE ST. LO SUNK

The morning of October 25, 1944, the Battle of Leyte began. The biggest guns the St. Lo had were five-inch mounted on the fantail. The U.S. battleships had sixteen-inch guns while the Japanese forces had fourteen-inch guns. There were no U.S. battleships in our task force. When the St. Lo tried to respond to the Japanese ships, it was their five-inch guns on the escort carrier in contrast to the giant fourteen-inch artillery of the Japanese fleet. "It seemed to me that the Japanese were focusing the full fury of their attack on us. I know they were battering other ships in our fleet as well, but when you're on board a ship under attack, you feel you're on the receiving end of their full fury."

Early that morning, Ed was on the flight deck performing his duties. He was loading guns, hanging torpedoes, and doing whatever else possible to help our pilots get into the air quickly. The Japanese planes were dive-bombing the St. Lo. "Shells were exploding, bombs were dropping, men were running across the flight deck, and the smell of gunpowder and airplane fuel was in the air," Ed recalled.

As Ed looked out off the flight deck, he saw five or six enemy planes heading toward his ship. "They were Japanese Zeroes," Ed reported to us. The destroyer escort with the St. Lo opened fire. They knocked down all the enemy planes but one. The last plane was coming straight at the St. Lo. "I watched this guy flying right at us. He was about four or five football fields away," McAteer recalled. As Ed watched, the Japanese plane dropped real low, just a few feet above the water. "What's this crazy guy doing?" Ed thought. "He's going to crash right into our ship." (No one had heard of Kamikazes before.) The plane kept coming and coming. By now McAteer could hear the whine of the engine and read the decals on the plane. "He's going to hit us!" Ed yelled out as he watched all this from the St. Lo's flight deck.

The Japanese pilot slammed into the St. Lo. It was a dream hit from the pilot's perspective, for his plane struck at the exact point where an estimated 180,000 gallons of fuel were stored. There was a tremendous explosion. A fireball several hundred feet high shot into the air and the ship rocked wildly. "I was on the flight deck not far from where the plane hit us. I turned the other direction and began to run for my life."

When a soldier is in the middle of a fierce battle, they report seconds can seem like hours. Images are etched upon their memories that they never forget. As the young sailor ran for his life, he stopped for a second to look back toward the explosion. "Bodies were flying all around me. I saw the eyeballs of one man just melt in his head, and then his entire body collapsed as his bones just stacked up in a pile," Ed told us. "I also vividly remember seeing the Japanese pilot. When his plane hit our ship, he popped out of his cockpit and rolled across the deck. I'm sure he was dead, for his clothing and body were on fire. He looked like a burning cigar being driven by a strong wind over the St. Lo's deck."

As Ed ran for his life across he flight deck, he spotted a place where he could jump to the focisle deck. It was a drop of about twelve to fourteen feet, but away from the intense heat and exploding barrels of fuel. Ed knew he had only one chance to jump. He spotted the perfect location and leaped to save his life. His jump landed him in a safer position on the ship, but he did sustain a thirty percent disability in one foot that McAteer would carry for the rest of his life.

"My foot hurt me quite a bit, but I had to keep moving. There was a catwalk in front of me, so I ran down it the best I could. It was the only way of escape." As Ed talked to us that day, his mind was certain, his memory was clear, and his facts were accurate. But on board the St. Lo that day, nothing was clear. The giant ship continued to rock as ripping explosions of airplane fuel tore away at the ship. Noise, smoke, fire, and pandemonium ruled.

Bob McKeg was a butcher on the St. Lo. He was directly in front of Ed on the catwalk, exiting from the mess hall.

The two young sailors saw a rope ladder that descended toward the ocean. Bob McKeg started down the ladder first. "It wasn't funny at the time, of course, but today it makes me chuckle," Ed smiled. "Bob was going down that ladder just below me. He shouted at me, 'McAteer, your foot is on my hand!' I shouted back at him, 'Well McKeg, get your hand out from under my foot and get moving. This is no party for which you are cooking a nice meal."

McAteer and McKeg climbed down that rope ladder in record time. They came to a place where they could jump into the ocean. Once in the water, more explosions took place and fire was raging out of control. The plume of smoke rising from the ship was massive. The St. Lo was already beginning to list. "We knew she was going down. There was no question about it," Ed said. "We had to swim away from the vessel so as not to get sucked down by the undertow when she went down." Ed and all the other sailors in the water swam a safe distance away. Then they watched as the St. Lo, their floating home and beloved ship, rolled over and sank to the bottom of the Pacific Ocean. The ship sank in only twenty-eight minutes after being struck by the Kamikaze pilot.

Ed and others floated in the ocean for about two hours exposed to strafing attacks by enemy fighter planes. "Watching our ship go down was like a death," McAteer related. "That was our ship, that was our home, that was our pride, and now the St. Lo was gone forever." A life raft came by and Ed climbed in. After spending another three hours in the raft, the sailors were picked up by a destroyer and taken to Guam.

Ed McAteer was one of the tens of thousands of young men and women who were injured serving their country in World War II. Doctors examined Ed's foot on Guam. It was discovered that the foot and ankle were badly damaged in that life-saving jump. After a short time on Guam, Ed boarded a cargo ship. This ship took him first to Pearl Harbor, then through the Panama Canal, up the eastern seaboard of America, and ultimately to a hospital in New Jersey. Ed only spent fourteen months in the South Pacific, but he experienced combat and lived through the world's largest sea battle. "Looking back now, I can say two things," McAteer asserted. "First, I'm proud to say that I was able to serve my country in whatever small way I did. I love America. I always want her to be the land of the free and the home of the brave. Second, I now realize God's hand of divine protection was upon my life. Had I been just a few yards closer to where that Kamikaze pilot struck the St. Lo, I could have been that sailor with the melted eyeballs. Without question, I know God Almighty had His hand upon me."

The hospital in New Jersey to which Ed went was clean and comfortable. He was there nearly a month in therapy. His foot healed up quite nicely, but McAteer would carry a slight disability for the rest of his life. He still walks with a slight limp and a little weakness in his leg.

Ed wanted to get back to Memphis. In late 1945, that's exactly what happened. The young war hero had to check in with the Red Cross. Ed recalls, "A lady was helping me fill out all the papers I needed to complete. She was very sweet, but old enough to be my grandmother." She talked to Ed about the papers dealing with government compensation for his injury. "Oh no, ma'am," Ed hesitated. "I don't want any money for what happened in the war. That doesn't seem right to me," he protested. "Son, you served, you fought, you were injured, so now you'll sign," she responded firmly. Reluctantly, Ed signed the papers. That was 1945. He received a monthly check for $21 for the next several years. However, the most important thing was the war was over. America had won. Out nation was still free and great. Summarizing all his navy days in one terse statement, Ed told us with shoulders straight, "I'm proud to be an American. I'm proud to say I served my country during wartime when she needed me, and millions of others like me. I love the United States of America." Ed McAteer was awarded the Presidential bronze star by the Navy Department on April 12, 1946. He truly is a hero for his courageous role during World War II.

CHAPTER 5

THE COLGATE YEARS

As I drove to Ed McAteer's house that September day for our next interview with him, I began to wonder what we would hear from Ed today. I was well aware that our agenda called for conversation and discussion about his years with Colgate-Palmolive, a multi-billion dollar company, and Ed's early years as a family man. Anyone who knows McAteer well is aware he spent over twenty-five years with Colgate, a fine American corporation that supplies personal care products to millions of homes. But what I wanted to know and get to the bottom of was this: how did it all start? After all, Ed was in law school. How did this man move from law to toothpaste? I wanted to hear what impact Colgate had on Ed and how twenty-five years as a marketing and sales champion influenced him in his future role as President of the Religious Roundtable. One question I knew I had to ask Ed that day was this: why would you leave such a secure and lucrative job when you were at the peak of performance, you loved your work, Colgate loved you, and doors were opening for advancement to the national level? Why leave all that for an uncertain future in the dog-eat-dog world of Washington politics where many people don't survive? Why?

As we walked into Ed's office, he was on the phone. He motioned with his hand for us to sit down. When he hung up the phone he said to us, "That was Ariel Sharon's people. They're working on something and needed my help, but it's great to see you fellas today! Here are some Cokes. Let's get started." That's Ed, involved with key leaders from around the world, but always happy to see his friends.

"Ed, tell us how you got started working for Colgate. Where were you? How was the contact made? What was your job? Did you like it?" Ed related to us that the war was now over. Millions of young soldiers and sailors were flooding back home. There was an optimism in the nation. Weddings were taking place, houses were being built, and jobs were being created. Ed came back to his roots in Memphis. McAteer was young, zealous, confident, filled with boundless energy and ready to tackle the world. After all, having lived through a world war, entering the job market would be easy. Ed was still boxing and several were encouraging him to turn professional and make this his future for the next dozen years, but the young man knew that would not be his life. Finally Ed made his decision. He would attend law school.

The G.I. Bill was of great help to many servicemen returning from the war. Ed took his Uncle Sam's offer and applied his G.I. Bill toward an education at the Southern Law School. He began his training, doing well in his classes and enjoying the study of law. "I was really trying to get a job as an insurance adjuster during those early days at Southern," Ed smiled. "That would be good experience for a law student. It would also provide some courtroom exposure that would be so helpful." The young law student had his mind set in that direction and talked with an employment agency to help him in his job search.

There were hundreds of young men looking for jobs and careers in Memphis when the war ended. One day the employment agency contacted Ed and told him that Colgate was in this city and looking for people to hire. They wanted to know if Ed had any interest in setting up an interview. "What would I do?" Ed asked. He was told it would be a job in sales. "Sales? That's a long way from law," Ed replied. "Yes, you're right Ed, but we see in you the right personality to be good at sales. And remember, Colgate is a big company that will offer a good, stable income source. Why don't you at least check it out. You will never know until you talk to them if this just might work out. All you have to lose is a couple hours some afternoon for an interview." Ed agreed to meet and a date was set. Little did anyone realize the impact of that "check it out" conversation on Ed or Colgate. For Colgate, they would soon hire a man who would become one of their top salesmen for the next two decades. For Ed, little did he know he would happily give the next twenty-five years of his life working for a company he still respects to this day.

The interview with Colgate was scheduled in the Dermon Building in downtown Memphis. It was a typical interview. The Colgate representative saw real potential in the young prospect. (Ed was only 22 years old at the time.) McAteer liked what he heard from the company. "Mr. McAteer, I believe you could have a bright future with Colgate. Your personality is winsome and you present yourself well. Our company has good benefits and opportunities for advancements." Ed listened to the regional sales supervisor that day and thought about a career in sales. He listened closely to the discussion of advancement. (It's interesting to note that Ed would one day hold the job of the man who was interviewing him for Colgate, regional sales supervisor headquartered in Memphis.)

"He told me what the salary would be," Ed told us. "I would start at $175 per month. Now remember, this was 1948 and that was good money back then." Colgate also provided Ed with an expense account for all the traveling he would do. The salary package additionally included a new 1948 Plymouth company car. The car fascinated Ed. After all, the war was just over and new cars were just not available. The auto industry was still transitioning back to commercial vehicle production and there were waiting lists at car dealerships to purchase a new car. Here was Colgate offering a 22 year-old young man a reliable salary, an expense account, and a new car. Ed accepted Colgate's offer. "I accepted the job on the spot," Ed said. "I thought I would do this for a while to get my feet on the ground and put some money in the bank." No one imagined Ed would work for Colgate over 25 years and rise to the highest levels of company leadership.

Colgate decided to start Ed as a sales trainee in the advertising department. This training took place in Nashville, Memphis, and Little Rock. McAteer was enthusiastic, personable, and a quick learner. All things went well from the first day on the job, and within four months Ed received his first promotion. Colgate needed a good, energetic salesman in St. Louis and they tapped McAteer for the job. It was a large and important territory, but management was convinced he could handle it.

Ed and his brand new bride, Faye, moved to an area of St. Louis. Faye found employment at the large veterans hospital in St. Louis. She would also teach high school English at a public school during their St. Louis days. Ed told us, "I was busy on the road selling the finest dental crème found anywhere in the world. I couldn't have been happier and I loved my job." The young couple enjoyed living in St. Louis. Both Ed and Faye became Cardinal fans and enjoyed watching the team play baseball. They became friends with Enos Slaughter, the famous slugger for the Cardinals. He owned a jewelry store in their area of town where Ed would buy gifts for Faye. Their first of two sons, Edward, was born while the couple lived in St. Louis.

Although the McAteers enjoyed their home, friends, and work in St. Louis, they would not live there long. One day a sales bulletin from Colgate's national sales office in New York City came out that read, "Twenty-three year-old Ed McAteer leads the nation in selling our silky cashmere bouquet hand lotion." The handwriting was on the wall and clear for all to see; another promotion was on the horizon for the young salesman who was the national leader of the pack. Colgate needed a sharp salesman in an extremely large territory west of St. Louis. The base of operation would be Wichita, Kansas, and the sales territory would include western Kansas, eastern Colorado, the panhandle of Oklahoma, west Texas, and parts of New Mexico. It was a gigantic region with thousands of square miles and hundreds of stores to service. Could Ed McAteer, only twenty-three years old at the time, handle it? Colgate was convinced he could handle the territory, and they were right. Ed not only survived the Wichita challenge, he thrived!

The move to Wichita for Ed McAteer would be a significant move up for him in his career. It would also be a major move up for him in his spiritual life for the next ten years. We requested Ed to tell us about his move to Wichita. "I'd be happy to tell you," Ed replied with excitement. "It was one of the most thrilling seasons of my life and gave me a new purpose for living.

"You see, television was young in America at that time. It had not really crossed the Mississippi River yet. Colgate spent a lot of money on advertising its products. Since TV was not available, we used newspapers and took out many large ads. As the salesman for that region, I was given a large budget to spend on newspaper ads. Papers like the Wichita Beacon knew Colgate would spend big bucks on ads, so they romanced me.

"One day in 1950, I was having lunch with L.D. Caldwell, editor of the Beacon. He asked me a point-blank question. 'Ed, are you a Christian?' I thought, 'Am I a Christian? I sell toothpaste.' I answered Mr. Caldwell, 'My wife sure is, and she's a good Christian.' He smiled and kindly replied, 'Well that's good Ed, but I'm asking you if you're a Christian?'

"I had never been asked that before. Obviously his question was well timed because he did not offend me. He apparently perceived that he could approach me in that manner, and I understood his interest.

"To that time, I had never had a desire to give any kind of statement of my faith. But I knew that many times I had reflected back on that decision I had made when I was fifteen, always positive of its genuineness.

"When I struggled out a yes, he invited my young wife, Faye, and me to attend his church. We did go regularly for several months though never actually placing our membership there.

"These were warm, earnest, and non-sensational people. Under the solid, fundamental teaching of that pastor, a very self-effacing man, I began to understand the teachings of the Bible. I realized my privileges and opportunities as a Christian. Faye already knew these things and gave me full support.

"In a halting, stumbling way, I began to study the Bible on my own, and to clumsily witness to my colleagues. I soon learned the thrill of telling someone what I knew about God in Christ, quoting some verses that I had learned to appreciate.

"It was electrifying to meet a salesman in a motel room, and see him gripped by the power in God's Word. Experimentally, I did this again and again, and saw the convicting and healing power the message brought into the lives of men. I became increasingly convinced that people were interested, that God could transform that interest into certain belief!

"Such was the beginning of my instruction and growth as a Christian. I am simply a witness. That's all Jesus commanded in Acts 1:8. Just like the witness in the courtroom trial, I am only asked to tell my story straight from the top."

Another key to Ed's growth as a Christian was the little AM radio in his company car. His territory was huge. The highways in west Texas and eastern Colorado go on forever. Often Ed was gone from home for two weeks at a time, driving from town to town selling for Colgate. During those many hours driving between towns, Ed would turn on his radio and listen to Charles Fuller and his "Old Fashioned Revival Hour," a young, new radio speaker named Billy Graham and his "Hour of Decision," and all the Christian programs that were aired over the powerful station in Del Rio, Texas. McAteer's car became a rolling college and Ed's major was the Bible. This growing Christian had a passion to know Jesus Christ better and to help other people come to know Him.

One day when Ed was home with Faye in Wichita, there was a knock on the door. Two men stood at his door with Bibles in their hands. The young salesman invited the two inside. The two men were part of a newly formed church that was sponsoring a revival. One of the men was a lawyer. With Ed's background and interest in law, an immediate connection was formed. The men invited Ed and Faye to attend the special church services. The McAteers did and were profoundly moved during that week. One interesting note out of those meetings was this; the church had a contest to see who could bring the most people to church. Although Ed was a guest to the church, he ended up bringing the most people and winning the contest!

It's always amazing to see what circumstances God will use to develop the spiritual life of an individual. One day Ed called on a Rexall store in Fowler, Kansas. Ed told us, "I knew the pharmacist and his wife in a casual way. I was talking to the lady and telling her what God was doing in my life and how He was changing me. She said, 'Wait! Hold that thought. Let me get my husband.' She brought her husband back and the three of us continued to talk. Then the wife said to her husband, 'I think Mr. McAteer knows more about the Bible than any person I've ever met. He probably knows more than our minister.' I listened to her talk and thought, 'Dear God, here's a lady who's complimenting me like that and I cannot quote one verse by memory from the Bible." God used that conversation that day to motivate Ed to begin a program of memorizing the Bible that has continued to this day. As he drove in his car, he would have key Bible verses written out on small cards and memorize them. Today, he can quote the Bible freely and accurately. Hundreds of people can testify that Ed has quoted to them a Bible verse at just the right time that helped them through a life-struggle they were facing at that moment.

Ed McAteer was one of the best salesmen Colgate Palmolive ever had. He was often the top salesman for the nation and led the company in marketing frequently. Of course, Colgate noticed all this and kept a close eye on this super salesman. In 1957, Colgate had a position open in Memphis for a sales supervisor. Ed seemed to be the logical choice. He was winning contest after contest as field manager. Additionally, Colgate knew Memphis was home for the McAteers and this could be a perfect fit, but Colgate management had two big concerns about Ed. One, he was too much into politics, and two, he spoke too often about religion. What would Colgate do?

"My boss at the time was Art Clark," Ed reflected. "He was a great man and a good friend. I both admired and respected him." Mr. Clark was given the assignment to check out Ed's performance. Were the two concerns true? Was Ed's involvement in politics and with religion hindering his effectiveness as a sales force for Colgate? Art Clark when to a Walgreens in St. Louis that was served by McAteer. He had orders from Colgate to check out the concerns. Mr. Clark asked the Walgreens' manager, "How does McAteer handle your account? Are you pleased?" The answer he received was very positive. "Does he ever preach to you?" was the next question. "Does Ed preach to me?" exclaimed the manager. "He sure does. He preaches to me how good Colgate toothpaste is, and then he sells me more of your products than I need every time he comes in the door!" Ed was offered the big promotion in Memphis and he eagerly accepted.

Working for Colgate in Memphis were happy years for Ed and Faye. They were both close to family and relatives. It was the city where they had first met, their two sons (Eddie and Tim) were happy in their neighborhood, and the McAteers made many friends. It was Ed's move to Memphis in 1957 that really allowed him to get busy for the Lord in his church.

It is difficult to find out exactly all that Ed McAteer does for the Lord. He is much more interested in telling about other people's accomplishments and of numerous instances when hearts have been turned to God. It came to light, finally, that his organizational interest is long-standing and far-reaching. He made time in his demanding schedule to work through several Christian organizations. He regarded these openings as opportunities for witness expressly designed to exercise the businessman's particular abilities.

The laymen's division of the Oriental Missionary Society, called Men for Missions, used Ed in Colombia, South America in 1957. "Laymen and preachers spent two weeks visiting on the rivers among the villagers and townspeople. It was on that trip that I spent a day in jail with a Methodist preacher because we had been giving away Christian literature."

In 1971 Ed worked with the Wycliffe Bible Translators in Mexico, assisting in the technical and field arrangements for the translation of the Bible into some seventy languages. As a member of their board, he also geared meetings and banquets among businessmen to bring support for the work, support in manpower and in substantial sums of money. (He raised $10,000 in one area of the United States.)

"Of the 3,500 distinct languages in the world, 2,000 of them are not written down. (These figures are from 1976). These are minority languages, but we are talking about 160,000,000 people. Jesus told of the shepherd leaving the ninety-nine to find the one. This is what the Wycliffe people do.

"When you reach a minority tribe, and manage to communicate the gospel in an introductory way, the man listening wants to know, if God is so smart why can't he speak his language? The translators work years on the tedious task of listening to, analyzing, and reducing to text that tribesman's spoken language." There's no question Ed was "seeking first the kingdom of God and His righteousness" as his life's goal.

A FORK IN THE ROAD

For twenty-five years Colgate could not have had a finer employee than Ed McAteer. He knew his products and was enthusiastic about them. He captured nearly every sales contest and record Colgate offered. Ed's rise in Colgate was meteoric. High- level discussions predicted that McAteer would one day move to 300 Park Avenue in New York City (Colgate's national headquarters) and possibly be named to a national position. But something was stirring in Ed's heart.

Did McAteer enjoy his job with Colgate? Without question. Could Ed settle down with Colgate for another fifteen years until retirement and secure an executive job with a lucrative salary? Absolutely. However, Ed was a keen observer of the American cultural, political, and moral scene. You see, Ed would read the news of the day, hold the newspaper in one hand and his Bible in the other hand. What he saw and read stirred him.

What was going on in McAteer's mind? What did he see and feel in his country that he loved and had served? Ed saw the pessimism that was sweeping the nation after the Vietnam War. He could feel the anti-authority wave that moved through college campuses in the '60s. Along with millions of his fellow Americans, he watched the tragic events of Watergate and the shocking resignation of President Nixon from the Office of the President. As a committed Bible-believing Christian, Ed also observed prayer being removed from public schools in 1963, the *Roe v. Wade* case of 1973 legalized abortion in our nation, and there was a growing trend in America against traditional Christian, moral values. All of this soaked into Ed's mind and heart. It stirred him. On the outside Ed was ever-smiling, but on the inside he was ever-churning.

What would McAteer do? America would soon have a birthday and be two hundred years old in 1976. Ed told us, "I asked myself, 'Can our nation continue to be strong if we remain on the current path? Can I make a difference? But what about my wife and boys? How will I provide for them if I leave a secure job with a multi-billion dollar company?'" Ed was in turmoil. A Bible verse seemed to reach for him: "If you keep quiet at a time like this, deliverance for the Jews will arise from some other place, but you and your relatives will die. What's more, who can say but that you have been elevated to the palace for just such a time as this?" (Esther 4:14).

Early in 1975, Colgate invited Ed and Faye to a large corporate meeting in Chicago. Another major promotion was in line for Ed. Of course, it would mean more responsibility, but it also would bring a greater salary and visibility. Friends inside Colgate urged Ed to take the job. "It's a brilliant career move," they told him. "And remember, New York will most likely be next for you." From a business perspective, Ed's colleagues were absolutely correct.

During his twenty-five year rise in Colgate, Ed had accepted many promotions. Several of these required that he move his family. In all those moves, Faye had never said a word. She accepted the need to move and began to pack boxes. But this time it was different. Ed recalls, "Babe came to me one night. She was very kind and gentle. No way did she threaten or demand. That's not in Babe's personality. But she kindly said, 'Eddie, please don't take this promotion. I've never said a word about past opportunities, but I don't think this is for us. I don't want to move.'" Ed turned down Colgate's offer for promotion and maintained his position in Memphis.

What would happen next? What would be Ed's future? McAteer was the ideal age for corporate leadership – fifty years old. He was known and respected within Colgate across the country. He was being paid a large salary and would one day receive a retirement package that was second to none. But what about the moral direction American was heading? That would not leave Ed's mind.

As I listened to Ed relate to us the struggle he faced in those days, two stories flashed like lightening bolts into my mind. The first involved Abraham Kuyper (1837-1920). Happily involved in his occupation, he hesitatingly relinquished it to ultimately become Prime Minister of the Netherlands. Kuyper came to this conclusion: "When the principles that run against your deepest convictions begin to win the day, then the battle is your calling and peace has become sin." Was this Ed's internal struggle?

The second thought I had was a favorite story that Ed's good friend, President Ronald Reagan, enjoyed telling often. Reagan would say, *Back in the fourth century, there lived an Asian monk by the name Telemachus. The hermit lived in a remote village, tending his garden and spending much of his time in prayer. One day he thought he heard the voice of God telling him to go to Rome, so he obeyed, setting out on foot. Weary weeks later, he arrived in the city at the time of a great festival. The little monk followed the crowd surging down the streets into the Colosseum. He saw the gladiators stand before the emperor and say, "We who are about to die salute you." Then he realized these men were going to fight to the death for the entertainment of the crowd. He cried out, "In the name of Christ, stop!"*

As the games began, he pushed his way through the crowd, climbed over the wall, and dropped to the floor of the arena. When the crowd saw this tiny figure rushing to the gladiators and saying, "In the name of Christ, stop!" they thought it was part of the show and began laughing.

When they realized it wasn't, the laughter turned to anger. As he was pleading with the gladiators to stop, one of them plunged a sword into his body. He fell to the sand. As he was dying, his last words were, "In the name of Christ, stop!"

Then a strange thing happened. The gladiators stood looking at the tiny figure lying there. A hush fell over the Colosseum. Way up in the upper rows, a man stood and made his way to the exit. Others began to follow. In dead silence everyone left the Colosseum.

The year was A.D. 391, and that was the last battle to the death between gladiators in the Roman Colosseum. Never again in the great stadium did men kill each other for the entertainment of the crowd, all because of one tiny voice that could hardly be heard above the tumult. One voice – one life – that spoke the truth in God's name." Was Ed to be a modern day Telemachus, changing the course and moral direction of America? Ed was playing mental ping-pong, these thoughts volleying back and forth in his mind, "Can I make a difference, or am I just dreaming?"

Ed began to voice his internal struggles and thoughts of the future to Faye. "Babe, it may be now or never," Ed told his wife. No quick decision was made. After all, Ed's family, future, and finances were all at stake. He thought deeply and prayed much. Would Ed McAteer be another case like 1917 when the Russian Revolution was raging in the streets of St. Petersburg and in session only a few blocks away from the cultural upheaval, the Russian Orthodox Church leaders were safely and secretly locked away debating what color vestments their priest should wear? Would this be Ed's strategy? Withdrawal? Late in 1975, McAteer made up his mind. He had become a success; now he must attempt to move from success to significance. Once again Ed would serve his country and fight for his nation. Ed's first round of service was against a military enemy. His second round of service would be aimed at a moral enemy that was attacking America.

As I listened to Ed, I could still hear the resolve in his voice, though he spoke of events that took place over twenty-five years ago. Then, instantly, I recalled Ed's favorite poem, "The Secret."

I met God in the morning
when my day was at its best
And His presence came like sunrise
like a glory in my breast.
All day long His presence lingered,
all day long He stayed with me.
And we sailed with perfect calmness
over a very troubled sea.
Other ships were blown and battered,

other ships were sore distressed
But the winds which seemed to drive them
brought to me a perfect rest.
Then I thought of other mornings
with a keen remorse of mind
When I too, had left the moorings
with His presence there behind;
So I think I know the secret
learned from many a troubled way,
You must seek God in the morning
if you want Him through the day.

Ed had met God in the morning, and now his life would be changing course because the Lord was at the helm of Ship McAteer.

Ed and America have a love relationship that extends back to his boyhood days of age twelve. Now he had to see if he could make a difference in our country's moral climate. Ed knew his future would be uncertain, but he was content with that. "For myself, I love to live in the throes, even the fierceness, of reality. That's the boxer in me. I want to be where the action is, where the world is happening. And that's with people." It was January 1, 1976. It was a new year both on the calendar and in Ed's life. America and the world would be effected by the decision Ed and Faye McAteer announced on that day.

CHAPTER 6

ED MCATEER AND HIS PEERS

"I will always be grateful to Ed for his early support. I have great respect for his faith and outreach that has helped so many people."

- President George H.W. Bush
41st President of the United States

"When the history of the Religious Right and its remarkable contribution to the political life of the country is written, no doubt there will be names such as Falwell and Criswell and Robertson and Robison and many others. But the one name without which there would have been no Religious Right is that of Ed McAteer.

"I met Ed through Howard Phillips. Ed told me he had been with Colgate Palmolive Company for many years and had made it his business to get to know all the key figures in the world of fundamentalist and evangelical Christians. He told me I had to get to know them as well and to convince them to enter politics and that he would go with me to make that possible. I must say, I was highly skeptical.

"Then Ed and I flew down to Virginia Beach and had dinner with Pat Robertson. He arranged a special meeting with Jerry Falwell, the meeting where the Moral Majority was born. He introduced me to James Robison who in turn introduced me to 12,000 of his closest friends.

"Ed set up Policy Briefings around the country to educate the new Religious Right movement on the issues of the day. He didn't just talk about abortion and school prayer. He had military people tell of our strategic weakness at the time. He had economists talk about the way to get the nation moving again. My colleagues and I preached politics. Ed packed more people into these briefings than anyone had done before or has done since. He significantly tested the bladder capabilities of these new recruits to the political world. We followed him from one end of the country to the other. It was exciting!

"Truly, there would have been no Religious Right without Ed. Others often get the credit, but Ed deserves much. God one day, I believe, will say of what Ed has accomplished: 'Well done, good and faithful servant.'"

- Paul Weyrich
Chairman and Founder, Free Congress Foundation

"Ed McAteer was an indispensable factor in the rise of the conservative movement and especially in the election of Ronald Reagan as President in 1980. The religious coalition Ed put together in Dallas for Reagan in 1980 was one of the most important events in modern politics."

- Phyllis Schlafly
President, Eagle Forum

"I have known Ed McAteer since the years of the Reagan administration and have seen for myself that he has been a faithful soldier in the army of the Almighty God. I have also found Him to be a fearless warrior in the patriot's fight to preserve the liberties established for us by our forefathers.

"Having been a soldier myself, the greatest compliment I could give to my friend is this: 'If I had to choose a commanding officer to lead me into battle against all odds, I would choose Eddie McAteer.'"

- RICHARD HEADRICK
FRIENDS OF THE LION OF THE TRIBE OF JUDAH

"There are those who had called Ed McAteer the father of modern Christian Zionism, and there is no doubt that he has been the preeminent pioneer of building support for Zionism and Israel among American Christians. The Prayer Breakfasts he organizes is a crucial demonstration of Christian support for Israel, and bridges he has built between the American and Jewish community and Christian Zionism play a vital role in maintaining and spreading support for Israel in the United States. Ed has brought together Jews and Christians to advance a sacred goal: the territorial integrity of the State of Israel. What could possibly be more important than that?"

- HERBERT ZWEIBON
CHAIRMAN, AMERICANS FOR A SAFE ISRAEL

"I have known Ed McAteer for twenty years. As a conservative Christian political activist, I have followed his efforts over the years to organize and energize the Christian community on a wide variety of issues. Indeed, he is one of the founders of what the media termed the Christian Right. He is a tireless champion for Israel and is everywhere organizing

Christians to stand behind Israel. He will certainly go down in history as one of America's strongest defenders of our Judeo-Christian heritage."

-STEVE BALDWIN
EXECUTIVE DIRECTOR, COUNCIL FOR NATIONAL POLICY

"When I became aware of Ed McAteer, he was a Christian lay leader with red hair. I first met him when I was a candidate for the local board of education. I saw that he was burdened that our nation was drifting away from God. Then he put legs on his faith and organized Christians to unite for God's work. His hallmark is that he never waivers. He is the same regardless of the storm, challenges, or opposition. He serves the Lord – straight ahead. His witness in his public life and private life is flawless. He is an inspiring friend."

-WILLIAM RAY INGRAM
JUDGE, MEMPHIS, TN

"An early experience in my acquaintance with Ed McAteer left a lasting impression.

In the late 70s, Ed was thinking about leaving a prominent and secure sales position with the Colgate-Palmolive Company. He was considering public policy work with a Christian ministry. Such a mid-life job change with its uncertainties would have been daunting to anyone. Ed feared neither the challenge nor the instability such a change might bring. His greatest concern was knowing if it was the Lord's will for him.

"That's when he called. 'John,' I remember him saying, 'you're a person who understands prayer. I want to come and see you. I need you to pray with me concerning a big decision.'

"Some years earlier, in addition to heading up a manufacturing company in Ohio, I had helped found a prayer organization, Intercessors for America. IFA sought to focus prayer on our nation and its leaders. I suspect this is how Ed became aware of me and tracked me down.

"I mildly protested the unusual request. 'Ed,' you're in Memphis. Do you mean you want to fly to Cleveland so I can pray with you? How about over the phone?'

"Well, this former Golden Glove boxer, this decorated veteran of WWII, this super toothpaste salesman wasn't going to be easily persuaded. So came he did, and indeed we prayed.

"But we also talked, and Ed shared his deep concern for our nation. I saw a brand of patriotism, joined with Christian fervor I had never seen before."

"Soon Ed had the confirmation he needed. When he organized the Religious Roundtable I was privileged to be one of his first board members — and still serve Ed in this capacity nearly 25 years later."

"From this vantage point, I've seen him sustain his uncommon passion. Ed is uncompromising in his love for his Lord, and undaunted in his desire to see spiritual renewal in our nation. But Ed's brand of renewal doesn't stay inside the walls of the church. It reaches out of the pew onto Main Street and Wall Street, to your house and the White House."

"Early on, I searched for Ed's uniqueness. I got a significant clue the day one of his friends referred to Ed as a "people pollinator." The description is apt. Never have I seen anyone more effectively and unselfishly connect people, inspiring them to work together in a common cause."

"What a privilege to have walked these years with one of God's great men of the 20th Century. His legacy continues to grow, and will, no doubt, until the moment he's called home."

"Ed McAteer has been a great witness to God's heart for his people Israel. He has sounded the trumpet to the Church. His twenty-two Annual Prayer Breakfasts in Honor of Israel have been instrumental in drawing Jew and Christian closer to each other in this crucial moment in history."

-John and Wendy Beckett
Founder, Intercessors For America

"During the 1984 Tennessee Senate Election, my volunteer job was to run the local campaign of the Republican U.S. Senate candidate and I thought Ed, running as an Independent in those days, was going to take enough votes away from my Republican friend to allow then-congressman Al Gore, Jr. to win.

"Thinking myself to be an astute political operative and a pretty persuasive lawyer, I telephoned Ed to discuss why he ought to get out of the race and even endorse our Republican candidate. Ed, ever the gentleman, talked at length with me about politics and did not waiver – there is no shifting sand with this man.

"Over the ensuing years, Ed and I have become good friends and have worked together in such common efforts as traditional family values and America's relationship with Israel. When it comes to the political side of these two important subjects, they have no better friend in American today than Ed McAteer."

- Ed Bryant
U.S. Congressman, Tennessee

"I met Ed McAteer in 1980, when he dedicated his considerable talents to the task of helping to awaken the Christian community to go to the polls and vote for Ronald Reagan. Thousands of us responded to his call to establish the Religious Roundtable and together with the Moral Majority they had a profound affect on that year's election. I shudder to think what the world would be like had it not been for the Reagan years in the White House.

"I thank God for the enormous contribution Ed has made in perpetuating religious freedom for America and for how he has led the way in using that freedom to advance the kingdom of God."

- Tim LaHaye
Author, Minister, Educator

"I first met Ed McAteer at the Louisiana Baptist University. We were both receiving Honorary Doctorates and Ed was the keynote speaker. I was immediately captivated. It was more than just his message, his charisma drew me in like a moth to the flame. Ed is infectious! I also learned that Ed was very accessible, which is rare for someone of his status and busy schedule. We exchanged business cards and discussed briefly how much we had in common and thus began a relationship, which developed into a friendship. We became Brothers in Arms for our Lord and Country.

"I've been in many meetings with Ed over the past ten years; spoke on many agendas with him across the breadth of America. It's always been a habit of mine to take the time on my return flight home from such an engagement to collect my thoughts and recap my trip in a journal I keep. Three things always stand out after spending any time with Ed McAteer. 1) I feel encouraged with a renewed energy to do the greater good for God and Country. 2) I'm spiritually recharged to spread the Gospel of Jesus Christ. 3) I'm physically drained. Ed will wear you out.

"God has given Ed such energy and sense of urgency. Ed is my dear friend and mentor. Ed McAteer is a true American Patriot. He is a troubadour of conservative thoughts and common sense. He is a trumpeter for the Gospel of Jesus Christ. Ed is an original."

- Terry D. Davis
President, U.S. Merit

"I became acquainted with Ed McAteer in the early 70's when he served as Interim Pastor at my church. After listening to his teaching of God's Word with great zeal and passion, I knew that God had sent us one of His very special men. It has been a privilege that the Lord has given me to know this great man of God and his precious wife Faye."

- Bill Anderson
President, Anderson Electric Company

"I have known Mr. Ed McAteer for many years now. It seems that our first meeting was somewhat accidental and that he simply appeared at an AIPAC meeting held here in Memphis. He expressed himself in such a sincere and energetic fashion that he immediately ingratiated himself with the audience. Since that time I have attended events that he has held in Nashville and Memphis, which he calls Prayer Breakfasts for the peace of Israel.

"Ed McAteer is a natural-born salesman. His business experience with Colgate has proven that conclusively. Even more so, however, he has utilized that natural friendliness that he has to speak on his own or for others in various settings that state stronger than mere words, his undying love for Israel and its people."

- JACK A. BELZ
CHAIRMAN & CEO, BELZ ENTERPRISES

"It has been my pleasure to know Ed McAteer, whom I lovingly call the world's greatest soap salesman, for more than 20 years. I have known Ed first as a devout follower of Jesus Christ. It has been my pleasure to work with him on behalf of the State of Israel and conservative political candidates and issues in America.

"There is a moment in time that I spent with Ed neither of us will ever forget. I was to be the keynote speaker at a major political presidential candidate rally Ed was promoting in Memphis. I spent the night at Ed's house. The next morning Ed started preparing breakfast for the two of us. Ed's idea of breakfast was a sweet roll about the size of a saucer, covered with white sugar. Ed tossed the rolls into the microwave and started one of his brief conversations, which lasted 30 minutes. As Ed is dramatically describing the day before us, fire and smoke start pouring from the microwave. Breakfast is on fire! I pointed to the microwave as Ed is warming up his subject for a second half hour. Finally, the smoke alarm kicked in and Ed perceived something was amiss. Now that the kitchen was full of smoke, the smoke alarm blaring, Ed snatched the blazing rolls and threw them into the sink where they were soaked in water.

"We didn't eat breakfast that morning, but the rest of the day was an absolute delight. Ed is not much of a cook, but he is a dear friend and a devoted Christian who has given his finest efforts for the Kingdom of God all the days of his life."

- JOHN HAGEE
CORNERSTONE CHURCH, SAN ANTONIO, TX

"Ed McAteer and I have crossed paths many times over the years. He always struck me as an exuberant, joyful, outgoing, and expressive individual. Although it was quite obvious he was an extrovert, it was also apparent that he was a very committed Christian and a consistent witness for Christ. He never met a stranger, and there was no one he wouldn't boldly approach with the reality of his heart-felt concern. Ed wanted everyone to know Jesus Christ personally.

"In 1980, Ed was focused on issues important to much of the Evangelical community, such as school prayer, the right to life, the need to stand against the Soviet threat and military buildup. Ed encouraged me to take a stand and speak out. I was quite bold in my beliefs and firm in my convictions, and Ed was convinced I had the ability to communicate these concerns effectively. He introduced me to many conservative leaders such as Howard Phillips, Paul Weyrich, Richard Viguerie, Jack Kemp, and Sen. Jesse Helms, and anyone else he thought I would enjoy meeting and interacting with.

"Ed McAteer boldly stands for what he knows, and he is unashamed of the gospel. In my opinion, Ed has contributed to the well-being of our country as much as any other layman in this country. He is a real friend for Israel, a real friend for this country, and a source continually reminding us of the importance of returning to the absolute principles upon which the nation was built.

"May God bless Ed and his legacy of inspiring us all to live fully committed to preserving our great heritage of freedom."

- James Robison
President, Founder, LIFE Outreach International

"Ed McAteer is an amazing networker and activist in God's Kingdom! Over the years he has faithfully labored to raise awareness and mobilize Christian action on many key issues, especially the support for Israel. His annual Prayer Breakfasts for the Peace of Jerusalem are perfect examples of his ability to mobilize key leaders in very strategic ways. Ed has been an effective pioneer in the growing movement of Christian support for Israel in the USA, and around the world."

- Malcolm Hedding
Executive Director, International
Christian Embassy Jerusalem

"Ed McAteer is a man of great character and faith with whom I am proud to be acquainted. May God bless him for his faithful service to our Lord and Savior Jesus Christ. I am honored to be called his friend."

- Judge Roy S. Moore

"I recall some years ago meeting Ed when he was trying to activate the Evangelical Christians to vote in the Presidential elections. So many of the Christian people at that time took little or no interest in politics and indeed, quite a few did not take the opportunity to vote. Ed's efforts have had a tremendous lot to do with inspiring millions of Christians to participate in the political process."

- Nelson Bunker Hunt
Businessman

"I met Ed McAteer in the 1970s when the Conservative Movement was just stepping out onto America's public stage. As conservatives, we needed a lot of things but few more than the knowledge and ability to market the conservative cause, as well as our issues, candidates and publications to a public that was disconnected and turned off by politics and even more so by politicians. Then this Colgate Palmolive executive appeared at the conservative movements leadership table with a vast amount of marketing/advertising experience and knowledge and he began to educate us. By the end of the 1970s people were very much aware of the New Right and much of the credit belongs to Ed.

"Ed McAteer brought many talents to the conservative movement, but his experience and knowledge is definitely under appreciated and was critical to our success."

- Richard A. Viguerie
American Target Advertising, Inc.

"I first met Ed in March of 1979 while I was Communications Director for James Robison in Fort Worth, Texas. We were planning a Freedom Rally that was one of the catalysts for what would eventually become the movement of the "Christian Right." From that point forward, I believed Ed was a remarkable and gifted servant of God, with the fire of a volcano, the energy of a tornado, and tenacity of a hurricane, and the kindness and authenticity of a gentle breeze on a summer day.

"By 1993, when I was elected Lieutenant Governor of Arkansas, Ed and I re-connected and it was my great privilege to speak at several programs Ed arranged. It appeared he gained in fire and enthusiasm through those years and had a fresh vision of believers taking active responsibility for their citizenship. I've often said I never worry about Ed making it into heaven, but in his enthusiasm, I do fear he might run past it!"

- MIKE HUCKABEE
ARKANSAS GOVERNOR

"Beyond a shadow of a doubt, Ed McAteer would have to be in my list of "Most Unforgettable Characters." The first time I met Ed McAteer was in the airport. He was waiting for me to get off the plane. I did not know him, but he knew me. He had a smile that would melt a glacier. He was full and overflowing with enthusiasm and his love for the Lord Jesus Christ was obvious. There was an instantaneous bonding. That was 31 years ago. I have never seen him let up, slow down, or waver to the right or to the left. If we could take what is in Ed McAteer and put it in the hearts of many more, our world would be such a better place.

"Ed McAteer is a man among men and one man in a million."

- ADRIAN ROGERS
BELLEVUE BAPTIST CHURCH, MEMPHIS

"In the late 60s and early 70s I, like many others in the U.S, was keenly disappointed in the crass immorality that seemed to be characteristic of our nation. Nevertheless, I had grown up as a rather typical pastor, convinced that the best thing I could do was preach the truth and point people to

Christ. Involvement on a wider scale was simply something that I did not feel compelled to do.

"At this point, Ed McAteer entered my life and began to prevail upon me to attend a meeting of the Roundtable in Washington D.C. and receive a briefing from others of like minded concern. At first, I resisted this, but finally attended a meeting in which, in a very graphic way, the devastating effects of the sex industry and pornography were presented to us. Having observed this first hand, I was left with no other choice but to become involved with Eddie McAteer and others in an effort to do something on behalf of our rebellious nation. I credit Eddie McAteer alone as the voice that God used to awaken my convictions in these regards."

- Paige Patterson
President, Southwestern
Baptist Theological Seminary

"Ed McAteer has been a special friend for more than thirty years. I first became acquainted with Ed during the late 1970s with the rise of the Religious Right. Ed served as an integral part in bringing together politicians and religious leaders of that time.

"It was during the 1980 Presidential Election that Ed and I shared the stage at the National Affairs Briefing in Dallas. Ronald Reagan was the keynote speaker and was seated between Ed and me. James Robison opened the meeting with a stirring speech that more resembled an old-fashioned camp meeting sermon. At one point, I leaned over to Governor Reagan and asked him how he would like to follow that. "Gonna be tough," Regan responded.

"It was because of Ed's great vision that such leaders could be brought together like that, and this vision has done so much to change the political landscape of our great country. There's no doubt in my mind that Ed McAteer has done his part to change America for the better."

- **Senator Jesse Helms**
Raleigh, North Carolina

"Ed McAteer is one of those unforgettable persons you meet in life. Full of enthusiasm, deeply committed, patriotic to the core, an uncompromising follower of Jesus and full of good humor."

- **Charles Stanley**
In Touch Ministries

"Since I have known him, Brother Ed has never been at a loss for words. In fact, he sometimes has too many words. In 1999, Ed's Roundtable sponsored a God and Country Rally in Huntsville, Alabama, and Ed was one of the speakers. The meeting was over at noon and Brother Ed just kept talking and talking and talking to some of the participants. The group moved out into the parking lot where Brother Ed continued to talk. As the clock ticked near one o'clock, many hungry stomachs were growling among the committee members who were waiting for Brother Ed to go to lunch. We tried to get him to leave, but he just kept talking. Finally, I went over and interrupted his conversation with the participants and gruffly said, LET'S TELL IT AT THE TABLE. Everybody roared with laughter. At that point, he agreed to a hiatus in talking. We got in our cars, went to a local restaurant where we got our lunch, and then Brother Ed proceeded to TELL IT AT THE TABLE.

"The truism is, all that is necessary for evil to triumph is for good men to do nothing. If America had more good men like Ed McAteer who would engage the culture, then our country would not be on a course of self-destruction through immoral activity. May God send us more Ed McAteers!"

- Dean Johnson
Attorney, Huntsville

"I have known Ed McAteer for more than 25 years and have found that his creativity, energy, and zeal for maintaining decency and morality in government has been an encouragement not only to me, but to a great many others as well. If every layman in this country was half as active and energetic in maintaining and restoring the moral and spiritual integrity of this country as Ed, America would certainly not have been through most of the ills that it has seen in the last quarter century."

- D. James Kennedy
Coral Ridge Presbyterian Church

CHAPTER 7

SEASONS OF CHANGE

By the end of 1975, the country had soured on politics and government. The awful stain of Watergate still lingered in the morning papers, the wounds of Vietnam were still gaping and fresh. The country was ripe for change, for a fresh return to faith and values. Throughout the year, Ed felt this stirring in his heart. Although still successful with Colgate Palmolive, his attention began to drift toward national issues, toward the upcoming election year. It became an overwhelming burden of urgency, a burden that gained throughout the year. Ed soon realized he could not sit idly by.

IN GOD'S PLAN, IN GOD'S TIMING

Earlier in 1975, Ed had met a Republican Congressman from Arizona by the name of John Conlan. Conlan had become somewhat of a rising star in the conservative movement. Son of a Hall Of Fame National League Umpire, graduate Summa Cum Laude from Harvard, Conlan had moved to

Arizona with the expressed purpose of running for political office, to align himself for a future bid for the Presidency. Conlan recognized a unique talent in Ed of connecting with people and urged him to take a more active role in shaping the politics of the country. Numerous doors in public service had already begun to open for Ed, no doubt due to his experience in marketing and his vast network of contacts. One such door, with a Washington D.C. based political organization called the Christian Freedom Foundation, held unlimited appeal.

The Christian Freedom Foundation was founded by Howard Pew in 1951 with the purpose of training Christian men and women to serve in public life. At the time of its inception, governmental office holders were prominently Catholics, Jewish, and some Mormons. When it came to basic groups like the Baptists, the Pentecostals, the Lutherans, these Bible-believing groups were absent from public office. Consequently, leaders like Howard Pew and the Christian Freedom Foundation saw the need to raise up and train Bible believing Christians to have an active role in politics.

In 1975, Rich DeVos, then President of the Freedom Foundation, began pursuing Ed to join his organization, even offering the position of National Field Director. By this time, Ed had made quite a career for himself at Colgate Palmolive and was nearing his retirement package. So, instead of quitting Colgate outright, John Conlan convinced Ed to go to Colgate Palmolive Headquarters and ask them for a one year leave of absence, enough time to pursue whatever political endeavors he so desired.

In the winter of 1975, Ed and Rep. Conlan flew to New York City to see Joe Herchberg, the Director and General Salesman for Colgate Palmolive. There Ed made his pitch, citing his friend Dan Kirkendall, who had worked for Proctor and Gamble, who had also been given a similar leave of absence. Ed was sold on the idea, anxious to move to D.C., anxious to cast his lot with the Christian Freedom Foundation. Herchberg on the other hand, was not so enthusiastic. He told Ed flat out not to do it. Herchberg asked Ed to let the Congressman go back down to Washington so that they could really talk things out. When Conlan had left, Herchberg tried to reason with Ed. He said, "Ed, you've done that thing down South. You've got the South in your hand. Now don't give up your career and your retirement. Don't make that foolish mistake. You're giving up a solid job and hundreds of thousands of dollars. Don't do such a thing."

Ed flew back to Memphis that week, back to his family. He was conflicted. He began calling on Christian friends and leaders, asking for Godly advice, asking for fervent prayer. One such man was John Beckett, head of the Intercessors For America. Ed flew to Cleveland that December, to meet and pray with John Beckett. Ed also sat down with his wife, to discuss matters. In order to make things work with the Freedom Foundation, Faye would have to give up her career as a professional schoolteacher and help Ed in the office. It was only when Faye gave her 110% support, never raising one word of objection or criticism, that Ed knew this was where God was leading.

On January 1, 1976, Ed McAteer, Regional Sales Director for Colgate Palmolive, called Joe Herchberg in New York to tender his resignation. It had taken Ed fifty years to make that call, but God had prepared him for such a time as this. Afterward, Ed called Rich DeVos at the Freedom Foundation and accepted the position of National Director, effective immediately.

PLANTING THE SEEDS FOR CHANGE

In January of 1976, Ed moved to Washington D.C. to begin work with the Christian Freedom Foundation. As National Director, Ed oversaw all meetings the Foundation had, most of which were held in the Washington D.C. area. He also developed and maintained meaningful contacts throughout the fifty states, setting up regional and state directors for the Foundation. One of the main thrusts of the Freedom Foundation was a political motivational film which they had shot and produced on their own. The film highlighted the basics of the United States Government, from the three levels of government to the electorate system and the workings of democracy. It also accentuated the many positive results of Bible-believing Christians getting involved in public life, of letting their voice be heard.

From the outset, Ed was awed and surprised by the enthusiasm his presentations received. He discovered something early on, something he had believed for many years, something few people at this time had adequately recognized; the Christian community was a sleeping giant; when awakened, it could become a virtual political powerhouse. It would be four more years till Ed's vision would become reality, till this giant flexed its muscles. For now, pastors and Christian businessmen and housewives and retirees came from miles around to hear what Ed and the Freedom Foundation was saying. They were trailblazers, the corner on the market, one of the few major political voices reaching out to the Bible-believing community.

Back in Washington, Ed began making meaningful contacts through the Freedom Foundation, friendships that would pay dividends for years to come. Up to this point, Ed was somewhat of a political novice, unaccustomed to life within the Beltway. He depended on these individuals to help him adjust to the changing political climate.

One such figure that would have tremendous effect on his life was an economic intellectual by the name of Howard Phillips, former member of the Nixon cabinet, founder of the Conservative Caucus. Ed was instantly enamored by his sincerity and his ability. Phillips had exactly what Ed needed at the time, political savvy. Phillips ran in the right circles, he knew the right people. When Phillips was going to meet with a Senator or a Congressman, he would often invite Ed along, enabling Ed to meet a number of important contacts. In the same vein, Ed also had something Phillips needed, that being spiritual insight. Besides dealing with economic policies and numbers and figures, Phillips had a great curiosity for spiritual matters. Ed recognized this early on and made it a point to try and win Phillips over to Christ.

Two other figures played crucial roles during this time; Paul Weyrich, considered to be the major force in assembling the Religious Right, and Richard Viguerie, the direct-mail guru who has often been called the godfather of the Religious Right. With help from such individuals, Ed was able to make the necessary Washington contacts, from policy advisors to policy makers, establishing himself as a fresh new voice in the growing Conservative movement. But there was also something different about Ed McAteer.

With his very first step into public service, Ed brought a spiritual fervency that had been sorely lacking in government and political life. He began holding Bible studies in his Washington apartment, inviting anyone and everyone with whom he had contact. Many of these public leaders attended, out of heartfelt respect for Ed, but also because of a genuine, rising hunger for things eternal.

RIPPLES IN THE WATERS

1976 was a year of progress for Ed McAteer. His transition from Colgate Palmolive to Washington D.C. had been a rousing success. The Christian Freedom Foundation was making positive headway in mobilizing the Christian community. Everywhere God had led, God had provided. The upcoming year pointed to even greater success. However, it was in the midst of this upward swing that God suddenly tested Ed, that Abraham experience, shaking the very faith that had caused Ed to venture out from security, accomplishment, and stability.

By the end of 1976, the Christian Freedom Foundation had begun to make waves on a national level. *Time Magazine* and *The Washington Post*, among others, had done feature articles on Ed and the Freedom Foundation, highlighting the organization's push to get Christians involved in the Conservative movement. Not all articles were complimentary however. The political climate had turned hostile and partisan in Washington, thanks in part to the Watergate years, still fresh in hearts and minds. The Christian Freedom Foundation, though thirty-five years in operation, had never been exposed to heated attacks, and the Left capitalized on this. There began a calculated attack against Rich DeVos and other members of the board. These men were all businessmen, heads of large and powerful corporations. Understandably, they recoiled at the bad press now being attached to their names. Ed felt this sense of unease at board meetings and functions. Although money was big and ample, these men could not afford the constant and growing barrage of bad press levied against them.

Consequently, in December of 1976, the Board of Directors voted to disband the Christian Freedom Foundation effective immediately.

Over the years, Ed had developed a pattern for living; when faced with difficult and unusual circumstances, be quick to find comfort and strength in prayer. It was to that place of prayer Ed journeyed in January of 1977, seeking answers from the God who had called him out into the wilderness. The answer came a few weeks later in the form of a businessman from Meridian, Mississippi named Jack Stack, who had also served on the Freedom Foundation board. Stack, a former oilman, now owned a company called CRS Industries, specializing in large air purifying systems. Stack called Ed that January and offered him the position of International Sales manager with CRS, which meant traveling around the world, selling the air purifying system to large structures like airports and convention centers. Stack also offered Ed the freedom and finances to continue doing what he had been doing at the Freedom Foundation, holding political gatherings and developing contacts when he wasn't needed for CRS. It was the perfect marriage, an answer to prayer. It allowed Ed to remain in

Washington, close to Phillips and Weyrich and the movements of the Religious Right. It also allowed Ed to see the world, traveling throughout Europe and Asia during the year of 1977. Once again, God had provided, meeting and exceeding any held expectations.

BACK IN THE SADDLE

In January of 1978, Howard Phillips decided to run for the open U.S. Senate seat in Massachusetts. Phillips called Ed in Washington with the good news. The campaign trail would require long hours and tireless effort, meaning Phillips would no longer be able to oversee the daily operations of his Conservative Caucus. Phillips asked Ed if he would be willing to leave CRS and take over as President of the Conservative Caucus, a full entry into the political arena, something Ed had been anxious for ever since the Freedom Foundation had folded. Nevertheless, Ed expressed reservation. As President of the Caucus, he would be expected to meet and discuss the passing of particular economic bills with Senators and Congressmen. He would be expected to address the Press concerning economic issues. Ed realized he was not equipped for such a task. He was a salesman, had been all his life. He knew how to market. He knew how to promote. He knew how to establish and mobilize contacts. This, he told Howard Phillips, was what he could do for the Conservative Caucus. Phillips still held the position out to Ed. Consequently, in early 1978, Ed resigned his position with Jack Stack and CRS and accepted the interim Presidency of the Conservative Caucus. Within a year, God had restored Ed back to public and spiritual leadership, blessing him with far greater resources and a far greater reach than when he had first begun.

The Conservative Caucus operated much like the Freedom Foundation, only with much more clout. There were contacts to establish and maintain, state and regional field directors to establish, and training conferences to conduct. So, once again, Ed McAteer hit the road, traveling the fifty states, meeting in hotel ballrooms and church sanctuaries, reaching working-class Christian men and women, encouraging them to involve themselves in the ever-changing democratic process.

One such individual was a young State Representative from Oklahoma named Don Nickles. Nickles came to a Holiday Inn in Oklahoma where Ed was giving one of his presentations. Afterward, Nickles spoke to Ed about his ambitions to run for the United States Senate in the upcoming election. Ed encouraged Nickles and even invited him to Washington to speak at a Caucus meeting. When Nickles won the Senate seat, Ed did his part to help the Junior Senator get acquainted with life in Washington. At one political gathering in Washington, Ed introduced Senator Nickles to one of the Caucus board members. The Board Member thought he was meeting a Congressman and told Sen. Nickles, "You stay in their son, and one day you'll probably get elected to the Senate." Ed stepped in to correct the error. "That's what he is. He is the Senator." Ed, always the consummate mediator.

PUTTING THE PIECES TOGETHER

By the end of 1978, Howard Phillips had lost his bid for the open Senate seat in Massachusetts and returned to the helm of the Conservative Caucus. They agreed that Ed would remain with the Caucus, now serving as an integral part of what the organization was doing. The two friends began traveling together, Ed assuming the role of promoter and organizer, while Phillips served as spokesman and policy maker. They were a dynamic team, enthusiastic and energetic, ready for something big, eagerly testing uncharted waters.

A group that would later be labeled the New Right had begun to assemble in Washington. They were political activists and policy makers Ed had developed friendships with over his Washington years: Paul Weyrich, Richard Viguerie, Bob Billings, Rich DeVos, Jerry Huntzinger, Art DeMoss, Senator Jesse Helms, and Howard Phillips, among others. These individuals had the clout to get things done in Washington. However, missing were the top Christian Evangelical leaders of the day, individuals who could get the message of morality in government to the growing mass of Bible-believing Christians. A marriage was in order, and Ed McAteer was called on to officiate.

The Washington crowd knew demographics. They knew voting patterns and swing issues. What they did not know was how to mobilize the Christian community, a community that still remained aloof to politics, skeptical. How could the Christian community become unified on moral issues? How could they be convinced to get out and vote? Furthermore, who were the Bible-believing leaders that could bring the message of morality in government to the church house?

Ed McAteer was the man with the answers. When Howard Phillips came to Ed looking for an Evangelical Christian leader that could resonate on the television, someone that could attract people to their message, Ed was quick with his answer: Jerry Falwell.

Jerry Falwell was a well-known pastor of the 16,000-member Thomas Road Baptist Church. He had also founded Liberty University, a leading Baptist college. But what gave Falwell appeal was his vast radio and television experience, namely his long-running and widely popular radio and television program, *The Old Time Gospel Hour*.

During January of 1979, Ed began calling Falwell, to encourage him to take a more active role on pressing political and moral matters. Ed managed to arrange a one-hour meeting with Falwell at the end of January. Ed and Howard Phillips traveled to Lynchburg and met with Falwell to discuss the movements of the Religious Right. Falwell was interested in why Phillips broke with the Nixon White House while serving as Secretary of Economic Opportunity. As Phillips began to explain, citing Russell Means and the Marxist Indian Revolution, Falwell suddenly leaned over and touched his arm. "Slow down," he said. "This is the most important thing I'm hearing today."

What was supposed to be an hour-long meeting lasted a full nine hours. Falwell called his secretary and cancelled his lunch meeting and any afternoon appointments he had. When Ed and Phillips finally pulled out of Lynchburg that night, Phillips leaned over to Ed and said, "When American history is written, this will go down as a red-letter day."

ON THE VERGE OF SOMETHING BIG

Not long after, Ed arranged another meeting with Falwell in Lynchburg, to discuss the next move of the Religious Right. This time, Ed and Phillips were joined by a host of Washington political activists and policy makers: Weyrich, Viguerie, Billings, Art DeMoss, Scott Stanley, Jerry Huntzinger, and others. Ed served as the emcee of the meeting, introducing Falwell to the Washington crowd and vice versa. During the proceedings, Weyrich was asked to give a report. He stated, "There is a definite moral majority of people in the American society, who if they were identified and organized and educated, would make a huge difference in the direction of this nation." Ed suddenly stopped Weyrich and asked him to repeat what he had just said. Weyrich responded, "There is a moral majority." Ed said, "That's it. That's what we'll call this thing. *The Moral Majority*." Falwell offered his approval, and the rest of the group agreed.

Given his background in marketing and sales, it was suggested that Ed McAteer direct the newly formed Moral Majority. Ed was not so enthusiastic about the endeavor. From the outset, the movement seemed somewhat isolated, with religious leaders refusing to mesh with other religious leaders. Ed held a different vision. He wanted to involve all people from

Ed and Family
1957

Navy days
1945

U.S.S. St. Lo
(Ed's ship sunk by Japanese Kamikaze during WWII)

Boxing champ

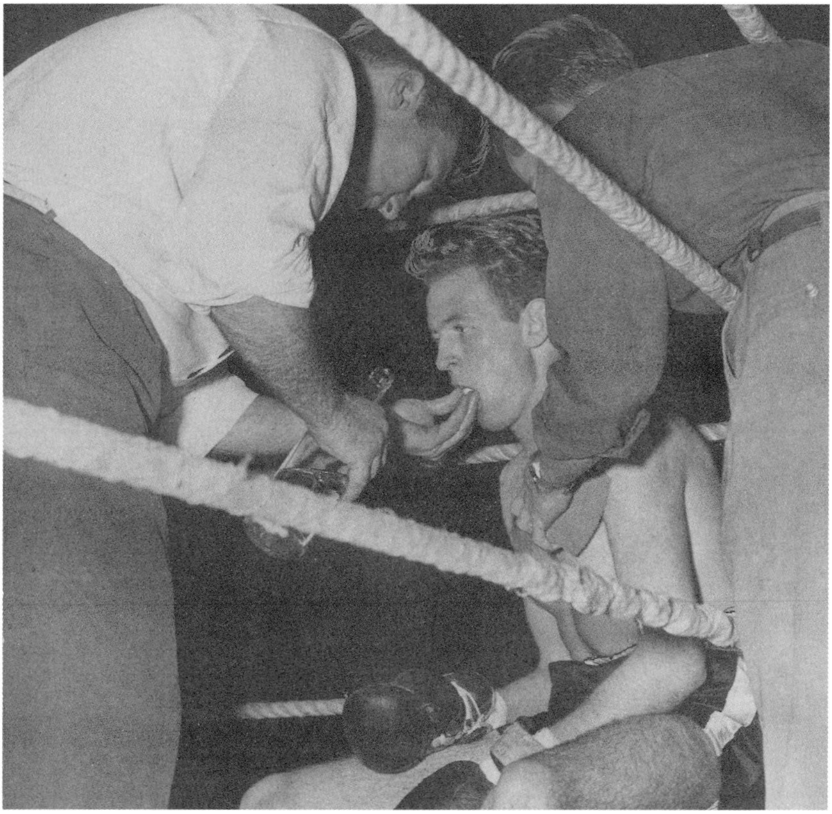

Taking a break in the ring
1947

Selling Toothpaste on the Road

At Home with Sons

Ed and Faye with Corrie ten Boom

Ed and Reagan in the White House

Ed with Senator Jesse Helms and Adrian Rogers

Ed with Holocaust survivor Nina Katz at International Prayer Breakfast for Israel

Ed and W.A. Criswell

Ed with Ariel Sharon and Dr. Moskavitz in Israel

Ed with Bush
1980

National Affairs Briefing with President Reagan

Ed and Faye with Dan Quayle

Ed with Attorney General John Ashcroft

Memphis Summit with Israeli Minister Natan Sharansky
2004

various faiths, ones whose purpose was not to convert, but to impact public policy on moral and social issues, to help shape the culture. The key was not theological congruency, but rather a unified front on certain moral and social issues upon which all faiths could agree. To do this, Ed quickly realized, he was going to have to venture out on his own.

It was during the formation months of the Moral Majority Ed felt that old, familiar stirring within his heart. He was still traveling with Howard Phillips and the Conservative Caucus, but there was a missing, spiritual element he could no longer deny. Ed was most comfortable in a Christian atmosphere, speaking with Pastors and Evangelists and lay-leaders. This was who he wanted to reach. His meetings with Falwell only confirmed this desire. It was time for him to branch off on his own.

Ed sat down with Phillips and explained his desire to start his own organization, one that could focus on moral issues close to his heart: abortion, homosexuality, pornography, and Israel. Phillips tried to convince Ed not to leave the Caucus, to stay on and help, but Ed could not be swayed. God had spoken to his heart. Phillips soon realized that Ed needed to be on his own and even offered to help. The two agreed on a suitable name for the new venture, *The Religious Roundtable*, drawing on King Arthur's Knights of the Roundtable, where every person at the table served with equal value. More importantly, Phillips kept Ed on the Caucus payroll, allowing Ed the time and freedom to properly assemble the Roundtable.

In September of 1979, Ed officially launched his Religious Roundtable with a gathering at the Twin Bridges Marriott Hotel in Washington D.C. Many of his Washington friends attended: Phillips, Weyrich, Stack, Sen. Helms, and Richard Viguerie. But also in attendance were the religious and Evangelical leaders that satisfied that missing spiritual element: Dr. Charles Stanley, First Baptist Church, Atlanta; Dr. James Kennedy, Coral Ridge Presbyterian, Fort Lauderdale; Dr. Adrian Rodgers, Bellevue Baptist Church, Memphis; and missionary Dr. Cameron Townsend.

It was during that meeting that the Lance Terrance Company presented their findings from an extensive survey the Roundtable had helped pay to have done. *The Attitudes of Religious People in America* reinforced everything Ed had been saying over the past three years. The Christian community on a whole was an endless oil reserve just waiting to be tapped, and unmistakably, the time was suddenly right.

When the meeting was over, there was a tangible buzz of anticipation, not only from the Washington crowd, but from the religious leaders assembled. Everyone realized they were on the verge of something big, an explosion that would soon be felt. Jack Stack caught Ed afterward. He had supplied the first $10,000 toward the cost of the Lance Terrance survey. He put his arm around Ed, and said with a southern draw, "Little Brother, I believe you're onto something."

It would take one short year and a former Silver Screen star to make it all come true.

CHAPTER 8

IS THERE NOT A CAUSE?

"It is no simple matter to decide just where a history of the Religious Right should begin," writes William Martin in *With God on Our Side*. "Understanding the movement requires some sense of what it inherited from its predecessors, and any discussion of foundational religious influences inevitably leads Americans all the way back to the Puritans."

He goes on to discuss "their profound and apparently permanent effect on American culture." The Puritans saw themselves as "a people explicitly chosen of God to create a City upon a Hill, a New Israel, a Redeemer nation." This conviction is reflected in the early documents: the Mayflower Compact, the Declaration of Independence, and the Constitution, and over the last twenty-five years has witnessed the rise of such organizations as the Moral Majority, the Christian Coalition, and the Religious Roundtable.

The adherents of this movement subscribe to the view that the United States is "exceptional" among the nations, not because of inherent superiority or goodness, but because of original intent. As the Mayflower Compact asserts, "We whose names are undersigned, having underwritten for the glory of God and advancement of the Christian faith do establish this first colony."

To those sturdy souls who survived the harrowing sixty-three day journey across the Atlantic, and to those who came after, the words of Moses to Israel might have been addressed to them as well:

"For you are a holy people to the LORD your God; the LORD your God has chosen you to be a people for Himself, a special treasure above all the peoples on the face of the earth. The LORD did not set His love on you nor choose you because you were more in number than any other people, for you were the least of all peoples; but because the LORD loves you, and because He would keep the oath which He swore to your fathers..." (Deuteronomy 7:6-8).

This sense of covenantal thinking has permeated the culture of the United States since its earliest days. There is a theological component to the history of this country, notwithstanding intermittent — if not unrelenting — attacks: Thomas Pain gloating over the prospect that "Christianity will be forgotten in thirty years."

Martin cites two challenges that posed serious threats to American Christians. "The first was the Darwinian theory of evolution, which constituted a direct challenge not only to the biblical account of creation, but also to traditional understandings of human nature and destiny, and even to theism itself."

A drama which played out in a small southern town in 1925 deepened the divide between proponents of the theory of evolution, and those who embraced the biblical account of creation. The far-reaching implications of that drama exceeded the dimensions of the event itself, contributing to the notion that conservative Christians are anti-intellectual and that the Bible itself is untrustworthy.

The Tennessee legislature passed a bill making it illegal "for any teacher in any of the universities or public schools of the state to teach any theory that denies the story of the divine creation of man as taught in the Bible and to teach instead that man has descended from a lower order of animals."

A young schoolteacher in Dayton, Tennessee, John Thomas Scopes, supported by the American Civil Liberties Union, deliberately broke the law to test its constitutionality, and was subsequently indicted by the grand jury for his use of an evolutionist text. The trial drew scores of reporters and hundreds of spectators who crowded the courtroom and spilled out onto the streets. Clarence Darrow, the colorful, pugnacious defense attorney from Chicago faced political heavyweight William Jennings Bryan, who prosecuted the case for the state. The brilliant and cynical H.L. Menken, dipping his pen in acid, "sent derisive reports of Southern and fundamentalist backwardness to newspapers throughout America and Europe," writes William Martin.

To no one's surprise, Scopes was found guilty. He paid a one hundred dollar fine, then pursued graduate studies and went on to a successful teaching career. But the damage was done. Protestant Christians and fundamentalists won the skirmish, but lost the war — at least in the public perception.

The trial itself became something of a circus. Christians were put to scorn. Darrow, an atheist, relished the opportunity to mock the Bible and ridicule humble folks who had no better sense than to believe it. Subsequent coverage of the Scopes "monkey" trial, as it came to be called, including the movie, *Inherit the Wind*, further distorted the event, caricaturing William Jennings Bryan as a hapless buffoon. Bryan, who was ill and not at his best during the trial, dying a week later, was no fool. He enjoyed a long and illustrious career, was thrice Democrat presidential standard-bearer and served as secretary of state.

The *Scopes* trial nurtured the discord between science and religion which was both unfortunate and unwarranted. The perception lent itself to the notion that the Christian faith may be untenable. Perhaps God is no longer needed to fill in the gaps.

"An even more serious threat came in the form of historical criticism of the Bible," argues Martin. "Imported from German universities into American seminaries and pulpits, this approach challenged the inspiration and credibility of the entire corpus of Scripture, the bedrock foundation of evangelical Christianity."

It was the misfortune of Protestant Christianity at this particular juncture in its history that ambiguity replaced certitude. The idea of anything being fixed, first, and final, was lost in a maze of pseudo-scholarship. What passed for "biblical criticism" was really a shabby unbelief dressed up in religious semantics. It weakened the great denominations, left its ranks unprotected from heresy of every sort, and robbed the culture of an authoritative voice when one was needed the most.

Another thing that adversely affected the culture was the tendency of some Christians to privatize their faith, to isolate themselves from the world. During the last quarter of the nineteenth century, that segment of the church that held a high view of Scripture experienced a period of intense activity. Thousands were added to the churches under the preaching of a former shoe salesman from Boston. Though never ordained, Dwight Lyman Moody led large crusades and advanced the cause of Christian education. Along with the upsurge in evangelism and Christian work of various kinds, a renewed interest in biblical prophecy took hold. As opposed to the view that conditions in the world would get better and better until the kingdom of God was established on the earth, "dispensationalists" believed that Jesus Christ would fulfill a promise to rescue true believers and literally take them to heaven, after which the world would be judged. Then He would return to the earth and set up His kingdom. Therefore, the task of the church was primarily evangelism: Save as many souls as possible in the shortest possible time. Moody held this position. He said, "God has given me a life boat, and said, 'Moody, save all you can.'"

This school of thought fostered a zeal for evangelism and missions and sparked a lively interest in "things to come."

Sermons were preached, hymns were sung, and books were written and read extolling the virtues of soul winning, holy living, and a daily looking for "the appearing of the great God and our Savior Jesus Christ."

You will find Ed McAteer in this camp. The overriding passion of his life is bearing witness to his faith. He has no greater joy than introducing a friend to Jesus. But he has another concern, often forgotten by those who hold this position. It is their failure to take seriously the role of salt and light in this present world. One need not abandon a well-reasoned Scriptural dispensationalism to insist that Christians have a responsibility to their communities.

Someone's values will prevail, McAteer asserts. Will it be Darwinism, which deifies man and renders God irrelevant, leaving classroom and laboratory without chart or compass? Will it be organized religion with its "higher learning," which has stripped the Bible of its authority and the church of its power? Who will write the textbooks and teach the children? Who will compose the songs and create the films? Who will craft the laws and shape the culture? McAteer argues that there is no such thing as a vacuum, and that if people who value the Judeo-Christian tradition withdraw from public life, others will take their place.

These were the issues that resonated with Christian leaders in this country thirty years ago, provoking them to educate, organize, and mobilize Christians, Jews, and other concerned Americans, encouraging them to let their voice be heard and their vote be counted. It would be a turning point in our country, and a salutary one at that.

First it would be necessary to unmask a myth. McAteer is convinced that the confusion surrounding the phrase "separation of church and state" is one of the biggest lies ever told, and it gets bigger with the telling (did not Goebbels assert that a lie spreads in proportion to its size?). It is well known to serious students of history that the words were never intended to restrict religious activity, but were enshrined in our documents to prevent the government from establishing a state religion. Unfortunately, the phrase has been bandied about so long, and used in every imaginable context, that the pliant public rolls over and plays dead when some activist judge frowns from the bench.

McAteer set out to unmask the myth. Resisting the politically correct dogma that consigned Christians to the closet, he would move out into the public square – and he would not come alone.

Ed McAteer had become increasingly concerned about certain trends in the country, from a biblical standpoint, as well as political, economic and moral. "I made my first little political noise in a local school board election in Memphis," he remembers. "I happen to live in a city that boasts more churches than filling stations, but I saw certain members of the school board making decisions which did not reflect the values of our people. So I got involved. I got acquainted with the board president, and together with others we let our voices be heard. I have always believed that you start where you are and do what you can to make a difference."

McAteer resigned from the Colgate Palmolive Company in 1976 and joined The Christian Freedom Foundation in Washington. He worked with them a year before becoming national field director for the Conservative Caucus. "All this time I was picking up a little more knowledge about the political process and becoming acquainted with people in government," says McAteer. "The big challenge before us was how to enlist the great silent majority of Americans whose voices were not being heard. When colleagues asked 'who is a tough guy out there, who is on TV and can attract people?' I brought up Jerry Falwell's name. He was the pastor of a large church in Lynchburg, Virginia. He had a national television program, had staged pro-American rallies across the country and was totally fearless. I said, 'He's got more brass than a doorknob.'"

It took some time to get an appointment with Falwell. "He wasn't sure why we wanted to see him, and he wasn't particularly interested in finding out," McAteer said. Finally, he agreed. "I'll give you one hour," Falwell said. Howard Phillips and I met in Lynchburg on January 19, 1979. I remember it as though it were yesterday. This was literally the beginning of the Christian political movement," McAteer said.

Falwell offered Ed McAteer a leadership role. But there was a problem. "Falwell, at that time, was an independent Baptist," McAteer says. "As a result of his schooling and background, he was not comfortable in circles not his own. He would scarcely have fellowship with a Southern Baptist, and he was disdainful of Pentecostals and others on the fringe.

McAteer saw it differently. He wanted to involve people like Pat Robertson and others who shared similar concerns. He envisioned an organization that would bring together people of various faiths, whose purpose was not to convert, but to impact public policy on moral and social issues and help shape the culture. Falwell had little time for broadly based Evangelicals, not to mention Catholics. Jerry Huntzinger, Falwell's aide said, "Pat will say an angel woke him up at 2 o'clock in the morning, standing by his bed, telling him what to do." This clearly did not mesh with Falwell's way of doing things.

McAteer's reasoning went something like this: Pat Robertson and I love the same Christ and are going to spend eternity together, so I think I can get along with him here. McAteer wanted to be free to go out and visit Mormon leaders, members of the Church of Christ, and others who love this country and are concerned about its future, even if they are miles apart doctrinally. "When I wake up in the morning," he says, "I like to have it fresh and clear, and not be reminded of someone I'm not supposed to talk to. People in the world know how to work together and get things done. Too often, Christians fail to do this. We have Lutherans here and Presbyterians there and Baptists everywhere who fail to understand that it is not necessary to be in agreement about every theological issue to form a common front when it comes to certain moral issues about which we all agree.

"It is important to note," McAteer makes clear, "that Falwell has long since abandoned his independent approach, and without compromising essential beliefs has gone on to provide extraordinary leadership. God wonderfully opened his heart and forged in him a leader who mobilized a moral majority in this country. He continues to speak out on moral issues, and always with clarity and forthrightness. It is certain that no one has ever doubted where he stands."

As mentioned in an earlier chapter God was leading Ed McAteer in another direction. "On September 19, 1979," McAteer says, "I called a meeting at the Twin Bridges Marriott Hotel in Washington, D.C. I sent invitations to many of the nation's prominent leaders for the purpose of founding the Religious Roundtable. There was a hunger in those days for such an effort. If I called such a meeting today, few would come. But at that time, there was a sense that something needed to be done. The response was amazing. One hundred and twenty-six businessmen, pastors and political leaders came. Among them were James Kennedy, Charles Stanley, Jesse Helms, Bunker Hunt, E.V. Hill, Adrian Rogers, Dr. Cameron Townsend, Phil Crane and others."

God-centered people convinced McAteer the reason for many of our nation's problems is the lack of involvement. He cites Proverbs 29:2: "When the righteous are in authority, the people rejoice; but when a wicked man rules, the people groan."

"Two other Scriptures have come alive to me," McAteer says, "and are part of the basic motivation for what we've tried to do. One of them is Hosea 4:6, where the Lord says, 'My people are destroyed for lack of knowledge.' The other one is 1 Chronicles 12:32, which provides a brief history of the children of Israel, then says, 'And of the children of Issachar whom had understanding of the times, to know what Israel ought to do.' Those two Scripture passages – 'My people are destroyed for lack of knowledge' and the men 'who had understanding of the times …' – how appropriate they are for today."

The objective of the Religious Roundtable is to favorably

impact federal policy by activating the potential influence of millions of Americans who inherited traditional, family-based moral principles, establishing effective lines of communication to them through the leaders of the diverse faiths and denominations. "Our plan of action," McAteer explains, "is to provide a forum for the exchange of information and ideas among spiritual leaders, organizational leaders and laymen on matters of public interest. We desire to foster spiritual leadership in recognition of the basic biblical principles and application of those principles to American life. If there is one word used concerning the structure, objectives, plan and purpose, it would be to educate.

"During my years with the Colgate Palmolive Company, I was active on several national boards, including Wycliffe Bible Translators, Teen Challenge, and a number of evangelistic associations. As a businessman and lay spiritual leader, I began to have the concept of what was needed, and looked for people who, first of all had a spiritual foundation, and then had some business sense. The Religious Roundtable advisory board is called the Council of 56. On it we have three types of individuals: elected officials, church leaders, and prominent businessmen. Among the original Council of 56 were W.A. Criswell, Ralph Wilkerson, Jerry Falwell, Jesse Helms, E.V. Hill, Tim LaHaye, Gary North, Howard Phillips, Ross Rhoades, Michael Valerio and Dr. Cameron Townsend.

The Board and the Council of 56, which is the governing part of the Roundtable, has been very careful to include a wide variety of participants. There is a Jewish community, a Catholic community, there are Presbyterians and Baptists and Pentecostals. "We include all these groups," explains McAteer, "because our focus is public policy, not doctrinal positions. That's a unique distinction. We have broadened our base while retaining our focus. We haven't tried to become all things to all men until we've become nothing to anybody. We operate on the premise that the majority of people out there are interested in what's going on in the country and want what's best for their children and for the future."

There is a definite theological underpinning to the Religious Roundtable. "I believe there are two philosophies at war with each other," says Ed McAteer. "One of them says there is no God. Man is the measure of all things. He can solve any problem he faces. The answer to crime, violence, anger, strife, is not spiritual. Change a person's environment and you will eliminate bad habits and misbehavior. The only problem with this ideology is that it doesn't work. The old Soviet Union is a classic example of the failure of this approach to life.

"On the other side is the philosophy that has shaped Western civilization. Its major premise is that there is a God. Its minor premise is: Man is imperfect. The Bible calls it the sin factor. As I study this, I came to see that every issue, whether economic, political or moral, is tied to one philosophy or the other. This is one of the differences between the Religious Roundtable and similar organizations."

If you ask Ed McAteer how he handles criticism, he will reply with confidence that he is doing what he believes God would have him do. For too long, good people have been ignored, have been made to feel like second-class citizens, and have determined to fully participate in what goes on in government. McAteer says, "I believe the great New England preacher, Jonathan Edwards, was right when he said that if God calls you to do something, you shouldn't spend a minute looking over your shoulder to see who's following you. So we operate on that principle.

"I speak from my heart as well as my head," McAteer says in summing up the ongoing work of the Religious Roundtable. "I deeply believe that every problem we face in this country is spiritual at its base. Until we take seriously such moral issues as abortion, for example, we will never solve other problems, be they economic or military. I do not have the ability to articulate how deeply I feel about this. That's why, in a society deficient in sacred salt, the people of God must recall the words of our Lord, who said, ‘You are the salt of the earth.’”

CHAPTER 9

REAGAN AND BUSH

Ed first met Ronald Reagan in 1975. Almost thirty years later, his initial reaction of the old Gipper still resonates: Ronald Reagan was real.

FIRST IMPRESSIONS, LASTING IMPRESSIONS

In 1975, Ronald Reagan had considered retiring from public life. He had spent nearly all of his life in the spotlight, as movie actor, General Electric spokesman, and two-term Governor of California. He had campaigned for Presidential candidates, from Barry Goldwater to Richard Nixon. He had even flirted with the Presidency himself in 1968. Reagan had been out of public office for over a year, busy writing columns for various newspapers, providing commentaries on radio programs, and even delivering speeches for large functions and gatherings. There were Washington whispers though, that Reagan would run for President in 1976. Some said that radio commentaries and speaking engagements were only preparations for a run at the White House. The Medical Association in Denver during 1975 was one such stop. Ed attended this meeting in Denver and met Reagan backstage. Though the encounter was brief, Ed left enamored with Reagan. Here was a man who was real and sincere, a man who stood by his principles. Reagan was every reason why Ed was leaving Colgate Palmolive to join the political arena. Reagan exuded true leadership.

By the end of 1975, Reagan had announced his candidacy for the Presidency, around the same time Ed had cut ties with Colgate Palmolive to join the Freedom Foundation. Though Reagan lost the Republican nod to President Ford, it would be four short years before Reagan and Ed would cross paths again, this time on the road to the White House.

DESTINATION, DALLAS

In 1980, Ronald Reagan won a hard fought battle with George H.W. Bush for the Republican Presidential nomination. Still, many Washington insiders dismissed Reagan as unelectable when matched against President Jimmy Carter. The reasoning was, Carter held a lock on the Southern vote and the Christian vote. What these insiders failed to recognize though was that the Christian community as a whole had soured on Carter and his weak policies. He had failed them domestically and he had failed them internationally. The Christian community was through with Carter infatuation and was looking for a new voice.

In 1980, Ed McAteer and the Religious Roundtable were busy planning a National Affairs Briefing in Dallas, preceding the election. Although they extended speaking invitations to both Carter and Reagan, only Reagan accepted. Ed sat next to Reagan onstage during the conference, his second encounter. It was during this meeting Reagan made the famous statement, "You cannot endorse me, but I can endorse you." The event was covered by hundreds of media outlets, including *Time* and *Newsweek*. The event helped the marriage of the Religious Right and Ronald Reagan. It also put Ed in close contact with the man whom he had admired from afar, the new voice of the Conservative Movement.

INSIDE THE REAGAN WHITE HOUSE

When Reagan stunned Carter with Election Day victory, many attributed the strong showing of the Christian Conservatives with the upset. Consequently, many of the leaders of the Religious Right soon became frequent guests to business luncheons and dinner parties at the Reagan White House. Ed's name appeared on the guest list frequently, alongside such friends as Paul Weyrich and Richard Viguerie and Howard Phillips. Although the meetings were largely informal and always rich with laughter, they usually centered around pressing issues close to the heart of the Religious Right. When asked about prayer in school, Reagan would reply, "No one will ever convince me that there is anything wrong with the little children praying in the schoolhouses of America." The simplicity of Reagan's message resonated deeply with those assembled.

One issue close to Ed's heart was the fight against abortion. Still lingering in the shadows of *Roe v. Wade*, abortion became a frequent subject of conversation. At one such luncheon, Dr. Jack Wilke, a doctor from Cincinnati, brought a large box of small tabs he had collected in opposition to a recent abortion ruling. He had them placed in the room where Reagan and Ed and others were meeting. After the luncheon, as they were preparing to go, one of the President's Secret Service Agents went for the box to carry it out of the room. Always conscious of his image as a capable leader, Reagan called off the Secret Service Agent. "No, no," he said. "I have to prove to these people that I've still got some strength left in me."

Although able to keep the mood light with his quick humor, those assembled knew where Reagan stood when it came to abortion. When asked about his stance, Reagan would reply, "The only people I've ever met *for* abortion are those that have already been born."

Nevertheless, despite his clear-cut opposition to this all-important issue, it was the abortion issue alone that caused the only major rift Ed would ever have with the Reagan White House.

THEN ALONG CAME SANDRA DAY O'CONNOR

In 1981, Ronald Reagan was faced with an open seat in the Supreme Court, vacated by Justice Potter Stewart, an Eisenhower nomination. It would be the first of three open seats that would fall under the Reagan Presidency. Eight years had passed since the Supreme Court had voted to legalize abortion in the United States. Reagan was now given the opportunity to turn the tide, in keeping with the views of his faithful constituency, and appoint a Justice that aligned with the views of the Right.

Slowly, rumors of a Sandra Day O'Connor nomination began to reach the leaders of the Conservative Movement. Their reaction was mixed. Elder statesman Barry Goldwater declared O'Connor to be a stalwart of the Conservative Movement. Kenneth Starr took a prominent role in pushing for the O'Connor nomination. However among the Religious Right, the response was much more tepid. In August of 1981, *Conservative Digest* ran an article portraying O'Connor as a definite liberal vote. The article echoed exactly what leaders such as Richard Viguerie had been saying for months, that a vote for Sandra Day O'Connor was a vote for the pro-abortion movement.

Ed began hearing these same rumors. He had spoken with a leader of the National Right to Life Organization who had met with Reagan during the 1980 Election. Reagan had told her, if you can get your people to support me, I'll commit myself to you. I will not appoint a pro-abortion judge. Still, O'Connor had voted in favor of a pro-abortion law while serving as an Arizona State Legislator. Ed became concerned. When he learned that a leading Christian Conservative Senator had stacked arms with the Reagan White House, agreeing not to speak out against the O'Connor nomination, Ed knew something had to be done. As he drove home on the Washington Parkway, he suddenly began to weep. He prayed, "Lord, with your help, I'm going to oppose this nomination."

Ed began plans to hold a Dallas rally opposing the O'Connor nomination. Immediately, word of this reached the White House. Ed Meece, Attorney General, called Ed to his office to ask him not to go through with this. Ed listened and explained, although it was not an easy thing to do, it had to be done. "You know how much I admire the President," he said. "But you can take my head off when it comes to me ever selling out my Savior. You can take my life, but don't ask me to be still when it comes to an important cause. I've got all the information I need. I know where Sandra Day O'Connor stands. I've raised thirty-thousand dollars to oppose this nomination, and that's what I intend to do."

Ed blitzed the media early that fall, securing coverage through numerous outlets, including *People Magazine*. He held the rally in Dallas opposing the nomination. Despite the strong support, Sandra Day O'Connor was still confirmed and sworn in as the first woman to serve on the United States Supreme Court.

GEORGE H.W. BUSH: AN INTRODUCTION

In 1980, Ronald Reagan wasn't the only Republican grabbing headlines. George H.W. Bush, former U.S. Congressman, former CIA Director, was running a tight Primary race against the Reagan juggernaut. It was during this

Republican Primary that Ed, along with a number of other prominent Christian leaders, set out to systematically interview the Republican candidates.

A group of thirty Evangelical leaders met Bush in Chicago, at the O'Hare Hilton. Ed emceed the meeting. At one point, Dr. Lane Adams of Second Presbyterian Church, Memphis, asked Bush outright, "Are you a born-again Christian?" Bush did not appear thrown off by such a blunt question. He answered with surety, "No Dr. Adams, I am not. As a matter of fact, I don't really know what all is involved in something like that. It's not really a terminology we use in our church."

Ed was impressed with this answer. Here was a candidate that was both honest and genuine. All Bush had to do was indicate he was a born-again Christian and he would have had every Evangelical leader in that room in his pocket, but instead, Bush chose sincerity.

It was during a break in the meeting that a security guard called Bush aside to inform him that his campaign headquarters had been broken into. When Bush returned with the news, Bob Billings suggested that Ed lead in a prayer for Bush's safety. It was after the meeting that Bush stopped Ed to thank him for his prayer. Bush appeared deeply moved, seemingly unaccustomed to such praying. Ed left deeply impressed, thinking to himself, "If I can only get close enough to Bush, I believe I can win him to the Lord."

THE BIG DANCE

By 1987, George H.W. Bush had spent seven years as Vice President in the Reagan White House. Although serving under a successful Republican administration for two terms, Bush still coveted loftier heights. By the end of 1987, Bush had made his Presidential ambitions quite clear. Nevertheless, despite his impressive resume and assumed backing from

President Reagan, the Republican field was well-packed, ready to make a strong challenge at Bush.

As the candidates began to assemble, their attention turned to Ed. Backed by an influential organization, The Religious Roundtable, and equipped with an endless stream of connections among the Christian and Jewish communities, Ed became an attractive ally for any campaign. What transpired could be dubbed a bidding war. Calls came from Senator Jack Kemp and Congressman Bob Dole who both garnered *electable candidate* status. Both wanted Ed to serve as their representative to the Christian and Jewish communities. Pat Robertson, a close friend for many years, called Ed for support. He explained his campaign needed Ed, whatever position he would want to title himself. He could pick the name and the position, he could name the salary. Although each offer held certain attraction, none seemed to be the right position.

In December of 1987, Lee Atwater, campaign guru and top Bush advisor, contacted Ed about joining the Bush Campaign. Atwater wanted Ed to come to the Washington Press Club and announce his acceptance of the position of National Director for the Christians and Jews for the Bush Campaign. Ed told Atwater over the phone he could 'put-that-offer-in-his-pipe-and-smoke-it'. "I'm not going to have any press conference there or anywhere else until I sit down with the Vice President and see where he stands on some very important issues." Exactly two weeks later, Ed was seated in the back of a black limo, riding with Atwater to the Vice President's mansion.

Once again, Ed was impressed with the positions Bush held on key issues. They discussed matters Ed held close to his heart; the fight against abortion, the fight against same-sex marriages, and the return of prayer to public schools. A week later, Ed called Doug Weed, who worked for Atwater, and accepted the position.

In the South Carolina paper, *The State*, Ed defended his decision to endorse Bush over Pat Robertson and others. He said he was, "absolutely comfortable that Bush's defense on social issues would be agreeable." In the *Chattanooga News-Free Press*, Ed explained, "The Vice President has made it clear, he wants . . . to guarantee the sacred and equal right to life of the most defenseless among us, the unborn. George Bush is, I believe, a man of integrity, a man whose love of family, like his love of country, is not mere words."

Ed went to work immediately. At the Bush Campaign Headquarters in Washington, he was given a desk beside the Vice President's son, George W. Bush. Ed later found out that his desk had been moved at the special request of George W.

Even so, Ed was rarely in the office. He spent most of the early part of 1988 on the road, traveling from city to city, promoting the blossoming Bush campaign. He held his first major meeting at the First Baptist Church in Dallas. This would prove to be his largest rally. When Ed would arrive in a city, he would arrange to meet with leading Evangelical and Jewish leaders from the surrounding area. It was in this small group setting Ed was able to explain to Pastors and Rabbis what kind of man Bush was when it came to the important moral issues. "All I can do is take his word for it," he would say. "Now I can read people pretty good and Bush looked me right in the eye and said, 'I will not, as President, do anything to promote abortion. I will not do anything to promote same-sex marriage or further removal of God from public schools.'" The message soon began to spread, Bush was a leader the Religious Right could trust.

Still, during the early primaries, Bush seemed to steer an unsteady boat. He suffered an embarrassing third-place finish to Dole and Robertson in the Iowa Primaries, then managed a key victory in New Hampshire against a resilient Dole. Ed happened to run into Pat Robertson around this time, at an organizational meeting where they were both members. Robertson caught Ed before the meeting and told him what a huge mistake he had made by supporting Bush. "You're going to be sorry you went with Bush," Robertson told him. "I'm going to be the next President, you'll see."

By the time Super Tuesday rolled around, the contenders had been whittled down to three: Bush, Dole, and Robertson. The Bush campaign had been steadily gathering steam. Ed had done his part to try and swing the crucial Christian Conservative vote away from Robertson and over to Bush. By the end of the day, the polls had cleared the path, Bush had made a clean sweep and all but secured his hold on the Republican nomination.

THE END OF THE LINE

With key victories in the Southern primaries, Bush had all but secured his grip around the inside track to the White House. With Robertson out of the race, the need to wrap up Christian Conservative votes no longer seemed imperative. Ed knew his days were numbered. It was not long after the Republican Convention, when Bush received his official nomination, that Ed received what proved to be one of the kindest, most complimentarily letters he had ever received. Vice President Bush thanked Ed for his invaluable contribution to the campaign. Without his help, Bush wrote, they would not have done as well as they did in the Southern primaries. Then came the line Ed had been waiting for. The Vice President was grateful for all his hard work and support, but, because they were moving into the general election, a reorganization was in order. Consequently, his position would no longer be needed.

Ed knew the motives behind the letter. He knew he had been pushed out because of his strong stand for Israel and moral issues. Once again, his faith had superceded the status quo. His service to God had taken precedent over his service to country. But did Ed McAteer have any regrets? Absolutely not! Let the record stand with his own spoken words. "You can take my life, but when it comes to me ever selling out my Savior, don't ever ask me to stand still.”

CHAPTER 10

ISRAEL, O ISRAEL

Ed McAteer is no stranger to controversy. He neither seeks it nor runs from it. Nothing has provoked more controversy than his efforts on behalf of the State of Israel. Since 1981, he has staged prayer breakfasts, dinners, interviews, press conferences, fund-raisers and other activities in a show of support for the Jewish people and their rightful claim to a national homeland. The effort has not been without cost. "I lost my biggest donors because of my unyielding support for Israel," he admitted. "When I first broached the subject with one of our board members, he said, 'Ed, Israel's got enough honor,' and shortly thereafter resigned from the Roundtable's board.

"I had another brother," McAteer continued, "who contributed between 150 and 250 thousand dollars in a two-year period. He said several things to me about my Zionist Jews having messed me up. When I asked if he was serious, he assured me, 'I sure am, and I've made up my mind as long as you do this, I can't support your work.' A prominent pastor, one of our first board members, was up front about his opposition to what we were doing: 'I don't share your enthusiasm for the State of Israel.' Another pastor told me that the land of Israel is just another piece of real estate. 'It doesn't mean one iota, not one grain of sand, doesn't mean a thing to God.'

"These are good people, friends of mine, but in some cases their theological bias renders them incapable of accepting certain plain statements of Scripture. The Bible says that God promised to Israel the presently disputed land from the time of Abraham onward. God said to Moses, 'This is the land of which I swore to Abraham, to Isaac, and to Jacob, I will give it to your offspring'" (Deuteronomy 34:4).

Ask Ed McAteer to account for his love affair with the Jewish people and he will explain, "The Bible is broken into two divisions, Old Testament and New Testament. The first 39 books are about Israel and the second 27 are about a man who came from that nation, whose name was Jesus. That's the story of the Bible. It's just as simple as that." He says he first discovered Israel through his wife Faye. "Her grandfather told her to be good to the Jews, citing Genesis 12:1, where God promises to bless those who bless Abraham and his family." Over the years, as a result of his disciplined study of the Word of God, he had become a "Christian Zionist." And he knows his subject. When it comes to the history of Israel, he is no slouch. He can cite dates, names, places and events. The story he recounts is simultaneously fascinating and tragic, a mix of victory and defeat, glory and shame, achievement and loss.

Its history stretches from the Burning Bush to the gas chambers, from the parting of the Red Sea to the death camps, from the glory of the First Temple to the horror of the "final solution." History will not last long enough to erase the memory of the atrocities and tortures of the Holocaust, of the roads of Europe choked with fleeing Jews nobody wanted and no nation was prepared to welcome. The last half of the twentieth century is indelibly stained with the shame and infamy of nations – including the United States and Britain – that sealed off escape routes and closed their borders to these children of Abraham.

The miracle is that this people has survived at all. "If you wait long enough, the historians assure us, the blows of time will eventually do their work on everyone. But the Jews were a problem," writes former Prime Minister Benjamin Netanyahu. "They received more blows than any other nation, yet they refused to die." He cites Frederick the Great who asked his physician for proof of God's existence and was satisfied with the reply: "The proof that God exists is that the Jews exist."

Addressing a joint session of Congress a number of years ago, then-Prime Minister Shimon Peres described Israel as a small nation forty miles wide and four thousand years deep. "Nowhere in the world is there a country like the land of Israel," Peres noted, "where so many weapons and so many holy places occupy such a small area." Mark Twain, who visited in 1869, was surprised by its size, "I suppose it was because I could not conceive of a small country having so large a history."

How small is it? We're talking about a little country on the eastern rim of the Mediterranean so small you can hardly find it on a map. Half the size of West Virginia, harboring fewer people than the state of Georgia, it has a landmass of 10,000 square miles compared to 5,000,000 square miles occupied by Arab states, a ratio of 540 to one.

This is the country, by the way, the European Union branded "the number one threat to world peace," whose occupants are assured that their future happiness and security lie in the ceding of yet another chunk of their national homeland to a neighbor sworn to their obliteration.

Searching the Scriptures and tracking the Jews throughout history, McAteer was struck by their uniqueness. For one thing, they are a mere handful, as Moses declared, "The LORD did not set his love on you nor choose you because you were more in number than any other people, for you were the least of all peoples" (Deuteronomy 7:7). Their influence on every aspect of human life – finance, statecraft, art, medicine, music, education, science, is strikingly disproportionate to their size.

In addition to that, they are a people set apart. The centuries of dislocation, deprivation, imprisonment, the threat of assimilation – and the wandering years, which saw their character maligned, their synagogues burned, their cemeteries defaced, could not alter but rather underscored the fact that they are marked. Try as they may, they cannot escape their chosenness.

In *Why the Jews? The reason for Anti-Semitism*, by Dennis Prager and Joseph Telushkin, the question is posed - Why? "Sooner or later, nearly every Jewish child, after a rejection, an insult or a beating asks himself the question. From the earliest Jewish history, through practically every era, in every country where they have lived and some where they have not, there has been hatred of the Jews.'"

Golda Meir grew up in Milwaukee where she attended Fourth Street School, and loved it, but she knew she was different. "And, above all, I remember being aware that this was happening to me because I was Jewish, which made me different from most of the other children in the yard. It was a feeling that I was to know again many times during my life – the fear, the frustration, the consciousness of being different and the profound instinctive belief that if one wanted to survive, one had to take effective action about it personally."

Two and a half centuries ago Jean-Jacques Rousseau put his finger on this uniqueness: "The Jews present us with an outstanding spectacle: the laws of Numa, Lycurgus, and of Solon are dead; the far more ancient ones of Moses are still alive. Athens and Sparta and Rome have perished and their people have vanished from the earth; though destroyed, Zion has not lost her children. They mingle with all the nations but are not lost among them; they no longer have their leaders, yet they are still a nation; they no longer have a country, and yet they are still citizens."

Byron lyricised Israel's centuries-long dilemma in *Hebrew Melodies*:

The wild dove hath her nest
The fox his cave
Mankind their country
Israel but the grave.

The yearning to escape the grave was illustrated by the remarks of an Israeli cabinet minister. Ed McAteer had invited pastors and rabbis to a luncheon in Memphis to meet with several Knesset members and their legal counsel to the United Nations. "We heard some country music," said one of the ministers, referring to an event the night before in Nashville. "There was singing and dancing. We had forgotten what it's like to be happy. We long to be simply happy. We want to live to see our children go out to play without fear – to grow up and not have to join the army. We have brought water out of the desert, built universities, and developed one of the best armies in the world. One thing that we long for: to live in peace."

The long journey to a country of their own, where their children could live without fear, where they could be "simply happy," began in earnest in the last two decades of the nineteenth century. A 36-year-old Paris correspondent for a Viennese newspaper, aroused by the growing anti-Semitism in Europe, took concrete measures to provide a refuge for victims of Russian massacres and mistreatment elsewhere. Theodor Herzl lived only eight more years, but in those brief years set in motion a movement called Zionism which would not end until May 14, 1948, when at four o'clock in the afternoon at Tel Aviv museum on Rothschild Boulevard, the Prime Minister David Ben-Gurion, dressed in dark suit and tie, stood up, rapped the gavel, and said, "I shall now read the Scroll of Independence." Golda Meir remembered, "It took only a quarter of an hour to read the entire proclamation. Then, as though a signal had been given, we rose to our feet, crying and clapping, while Ben-Gurion, his voice breaking for the only time, read: 'The State of Israel will be open to Jewish immigration and the ingathering of exiles.'"

Like the bush in the wilderness that burned but was not consumed, so Israel, pilloried, plundered, and profaned, refused to disappear. Rising from the ashes of Auschwitz, emerging from the torture cells of Treblinka and Dachau, and staggering up out of the sewers of Warsaw, they returned to their historic homeland.

Now that they were an accepted fact, the remaining question was how they would stay alive. By the morning of May 15, Israel was under armed attack from the North, the East, and the South. Egypt, Jordan, Lebanon, Syria, and Iraq concluded that the creation of an Israeli state was not a good idea and that it should be dismantled before the ink was dry on the paperwork.

By the time the fledgling nation had turned back the five bully states, some things had been pretty well agreed upon. For starters, they weren't going anywhere. Their collective memory was heavy with sights and sounds and smells and images too horrible to remember, too awful to forget, and they vowed never again to be driven from their homes to wander defenseless in hostile lands. And they certainly were in no mood to be lectured by nations that had refused them the time of day when their lives were in jeopardy.

Golda Meir said she would have been much more nervous when she met with the Pope on January 16, 1973, had he not started the visit by "telling me that he found it hard to accept the fact that the Jews – who, of all people, should have been capable of mercy toward others because they had suffered so terribly themselves – had behaved so harshly in their own country. Well, that is the kind of talk I can't bear, particularly since it is not true that we have mistreated the Arabs."

"Your Holiness," Meir addressed the Pope, "do you know what my own very earliest memory is? It is waiting for a pogrom in Kiev. Let me assure you that my people know all about real harshness and also that we learned all about real mercy when we were being led to the gas chambers of the Nazis.'"

The years that followed were marked by intense effort and unrelenting struggle. Survival depended upon finding water where there was no water, turning swamps into gardens, building homes and schools and universities, not to mention forging a government and building a national defense.

There were wars and rumors of wars. Armies massed on the borders, saboteurs and suicide bombers breached the perimeters, and too often, promised aid from friendly countries never came. But the dream expressed by Shimon Peres became a conviction: "We can wash this blood-soaked land of conflict with living water, we can grow flowers on the battlefields of the past and bring smiles to Jewish and Arab children – indeed, to all our children, who will inherit our land and live there in happiness and peace."

The cost of cleansing that blood-soaked land over the last half century has come at a premium, but a promise had been made to the dead and the yet unborn, and that promise would be kept. The reborn nation geared up for instant mobilization. Former refugees and returning exiles became warriors. Public parks were converted to cemeteries where twenty-one thousand fallen warriors lie buried.

The Bible says that a brother is born for adversity. Such a brother was found in the Mississippi Delta city of Memphis. Ed McAteer, the Baptist layman, would rouse the evangelical world to stand with the ancient people of God. Israel's Minister of Tourism Benny Elon calls the Bible the essence of a relationship between Israelis and Americans that runs deeper than mere political interests. He says, "There are differences between Christians and Jews, but there is no argument that everything started with Abraham, Isaac, and Jacob."

Unlike much of Protestantism, which picks and chooses when it comes to the Bible, Evangelicals embrace a high view of Scripture. The Lord made a promise to Abraham, and the Lord keeps his promises. That is non-negotiable. A few years ago, McAteer went to Israel and hired a craftsman to chisel the

Ten Commandments in Hebrew and English on a slab of rock. He carried that tablet up Mt. Sinai, and then descended with the Commandments in his hand. Upon returning home, he called then-Senator John Ashcroft and said, "Brother John, guess what I did? I came down the mountain, just like Moses, with the Ten Commandments in my hand." After a short pause, Ashcroft said, "Let me ask you, did you carry them up with you?"

The tablets Moses carried down the mountain were not inscribed by an Israeli craftsman but were written by the finger of God. Revelation, sovereignty, authority, certainty. This describes the faith of the evangelical Christian. So when McAteer was asked on 60 Minutes to explain his bond with the Jewish people and his support of their statehood, he answered as he always does to such inquiries by citing the Scriptures:

"Hear the word of the LORD, and declare it in the isles afar off, and say, 'He that scattered Israel will gather him and keep him as a shepherd does his flock'" (Jeremiah 31:10).

"He will set up a banner for the nations, and will assemble the outcasts of Israel and gather together the dispersed of Judea from the four corners of the earth" (Isaiah 11:12).

"For I will take you from among the nations, and gather you out of all countries and bring you into your own land" (Ezekiel 36:24).

To Evangelicals, Israel's rebirth during the twentieth century is no accident, but a fulfillment of Ezekiel's vision of dry bones that substantiates the trustworthiness of His Word. "America has a strong interest in the Middle East," McAteer says. "We affirm our belief that the nation of Israel is the key to that interest because of our common bonds, our common belief in social justice, and the godly principles on which our two countries were founded."

In spite of that common bond, it has not been easy to forge a relationship with the Jewish people, many who are suspicious of Christian friendship, fearful of their real motives. For Jews who know Ed McAteer, that fear is unwarranted. In the first place, his friendship is transparent. "His love for the nation of Israel is legendary," notes his pastor, Adrian Rogers. "He has more genuine Jewish friends than any evangelical Christian I know."

Another staunch friend, whose love for Israel was also legendary, was a little lady from Holland, Corrie ten Boom. "She was the greatest gentile Christian I ever knew," McAteer says. Her father ran a watch shop in Amsterdam. A hundred years before, Corrie's grandfather put the Jews on his special prayer list. In part, his prayers were answered when Corrie's father pushed out a wall in the family home and built a "hiding place" where Jews were hidden away from the Nazis, who at that time were hauling them off to concentration camps. When he first tried to shelter a Jewish baby, a pastor warned him of the danger. Mr. ten Boom replied, "You say we could lose our lives for this child. I would consider that the greatest honor that could come to this family."

When the attempt to hide the hunted was discovered, Corrie, her father and her sister were arrested. The Nazis told Mr. Caspar ten Boom, a revered Dutch citizen, well into his eighties, that they would release him if he would stop his activity in sheltering the Jews. Corrie recalls the scene in her remarkable book, *The Hiding Place*.

"The Gestapo chief leaned forward, 'I'd like to send you home, old fellow,' he said. 'I'll take your word that you won't cause any more trouble.'

"If I go home today, he said evenly and clearly, 'tomorrow I will open my door again to any man in need who knocks.'"

Shortly thereafter, the old man died in isolation and the sisters were shipped off to Ravensbruck. Corrie alone survived the filth and horror of the camps. On three occasions, she was marked for death, but some mix-up resulted in her release.

She once said, "When you stand before the gas chamber, you're stripped naked and ready to walk in to die, things become very simple. In fact there are only two things on your mind, life or death."

"I met her when she came to this country back in the sixties," McAteer says. "She was with Billy Graham in Atlanta. I flew down and told her about our work with the Jewish people and invited her to Memphis. A German girl, her traveling companion, listened for a while and said, 'No, I don't think we can work that into our schedule.' Then Corrie said, 'Ellen, I think we go.'" They came and spent several days with the McAteers. Several meetings were held including a great rally in the Ellis Auditorium. "The impact on the city of Memphis and the Jewish community was terrific. Here was a gentile family who had risked their lives for their Jewish neighbors. She had hardly started talking when a policeman went out just sobbing. She had the touch of God on her," McAteer says.

"Ed, you have no idea how this reaches the heart of a Holocaust survivor," said Nina Katz, herself a survivor. This was only twenty years after the Holocaust, the horror of which was still fresh in the memory of many to whom Hitler was a baptized "Christian." Corrie ten Boom tramped the world sharing the love of her Savior to Jew and gentile alike. Few people in the twentieth century did more to bridge the gap between Christian and Jew.

The word "Christian" is the most abused and misunderstood word in any language, McAteer insists. "It has come to designate anyone not a Hindu or Buddhist or atheist. The word conjures up images of the Crusaders sweeping the countryside pillaging and raping and killing. Our carelessness has almost emptied the word of any meaning. An evangelical Christian is one who is born again, who takes the Bible seriously, and who loves the Savior. This "born again" message demands a peculiar relationship with the people of Israel. The forefathers of today's Evangelicals saw themselves in covenant relationship with God similar to Israel's destiny, rebirth and security. Out of this uniquely prophetic expression of solidarity was born the National Prayer Breakfast in Honor of Israel.

Encouraged by its executive director, Dr. Ben Armstrong,

the breakfast was launched by McAteer's Religious Roundtable and elements within the National Religious Broadcasters. The first breakfast was held at the Shoreham Hotel in Washington, D.C. in 1981. Fifteen hundred packed the ballroom to hear religious and political leaders as well as guests from the State of Israel. One of the speakers was Jerry Falwell, who said; "I think this is the greatest meeting I've ever attended in my life – Christians expressing their love and honor for the Jews."

"A funny thing happened on our way to the first prayer breakfast," McAteer remembers. "At 1:30 in the morning, I was sitting in my room making notes for the meeting when I heard a voice say, 'No, no, the prayer breakfast is not canceled.' I opened the door and found this little lady and her husband, missionaries to Israel. They had gotten out of bed on an impulse just as a slip of paper was slid under the door. It said, 'Prayer Breakfast Canceled.' She opened the door and saw the guy who had delivered the note, and was protesting, 'No, no, it's not canceled.'

"She called me and we headed for the elevator where we ran into this big brute of a guy who called himself a 'black Hebrew'. He said, 'If you get on here, you won't get off alive.' We ran downstairs and discovered they had set up a phone bank and were calling around, saying that the breakfast was canceled.

"I said, boy, what are we going to do? I said we've got to get something under these doors. We found an all-night print shop and printed a flyer. It read: 'It's a lie!' We printed it and went to every room in the middle of the night. The crowd the next morning was standing room only. Dr. Stephen Olford brought the devotions and Ed Meese spoke, and his subject, I'll never forget it, was 'terrorism.'

"That was not the last time the devil overplayed his hand.

"There have now been twenty-two prayer breakfasts. Speakers have included Kay Arthur, Al Gore, Alfonse D' Amato, Orrin Hatch, Jerry Falwell, Jesse Helms, Yitzhak Shamir, several Israeli ambassadors and others. Evangelicals confirm the Messianic destiny of both the church and Israel and believe that the Second Coming of Jesus will establish the Millennium. There is no conflict or compromise on their part with Jesus' brothers, the Jewish people. It is both a privilege and a divine injunction to befriend the Jews."

The Roundtable, along with an annual sponsor, has initiated an annual "Proclamation of Blessing" document that clearly states the purpose of the gathering: solidarity with Israel and support of world Jewry. It is a positive expression, not anti-Arab, nor a subtle form of racism. To the contrary, each year a call is made to renounce all forms of racial hatred and terrorism, especially among those within the Middle East. "We do not believe that righteousness and justice are in conflict with biblical fulfillment," Ed says "and that as Israel finds her place among the nations, peace, justice and prosperity will find ample and blessed room for all."

It is safe to say that Ed McAteer is fond of George H. W. Bush, the former president, and the decision to serve as national head of Christians and Jews for Bush in 1988 was not difficult to make. "George Bush is a man of integrity, a man whose love of country is not mere words. It is plain to see, and a matter of record. He appreciates the precious heritage of America's traditional Judeo-Christian values."

After the election of George W. Bush in 2000, a wide array of conservative Christians and Jews lobbied the White House to get McAteer nominated to be ambassador to Israel. Letters of support were sent to Washington by Tennessee Governor Don Sundquist; Sen. Fred Thompson; Adrian Rogers, pastor of Bellevue Baptist Church in Memphis; Arkansas Governor Mike Huckabee; Judge Roy Moore; Rabbi Rafael Grossman of Baron Hirsch Congregation, the largest orthodox congregation in the United States; Rep. Ernest Istook of Oklahoma and many others.

"When the League of Nations, with strong American support, endorsed the concept of a Jewish homeland in Palestine in 1922, it did so on the basis of the biblical connection between the Jews and the land of Israel," Jewish leader Herbert Zweibon told the Bush White House. "You need an ambassador who understands that connection. Appointing Ed McAteer as our ambassador to Israel will send a badly needed message that those who appreciate religious values have a place in your administration."

Years before, Ehud Olmert, mayor of Jerusalem, suggested McAteer would be a good ambassador to Israel. Although the appointment never came, McAteer's priorities never wavered: "I'd rather be the ambassador to Israel than the president of the United States. The reward would be greater because of eternity."

Israel has never needed that kind of friendship and loyalty more than it does today. Ed McAteer believes Israel may be in more danger now than at any time since its rebirth in 1948. The United States, the UN, Russia and the European Union have conceived a "road map" to peace, which more accurately resembles a road map to ruin. According to Dave Hunt, author and speaker, "It ignores the fact that, according to Islam, Israel may not possess any part of 'Palestine,' which Islam claims was given to Ishmael and his Arab descendants, not to Isaac and his Jewish descendants."

The plan, among other provisions, would return Israel to its 1967 indefensible borders without any security safeguards. When asked about the highly touted blueprint for peace, McAteer wastes no time and minces no words: "We are going diametrically opposed to the Word of God, and no individual, no family, no nation, no civilization, has ever successfully done that and survived. In pushing Israel in this direction, the nations are defying God, who said, 'The land shall not be sold (or traded) forever; for the land is mine' (Lev. 25:23). The false peace that may soon be established is, in fact, a road map to Armageddon."

The struggle to retrieve their homeland was marked by conflict and fraught with danger and the battle to retain that homeland has been no less challenging. Israel is being prodded by the international community to deal with individuals and organizations clearly committed to their destruction. Take Yasir Arafat, for example. Long ago, Prime Minister Golda Meir described him as "a costumed multiple murderer heading a movement dedicated solely to the destruction of the state of Israel." In 1995, Ariel Sharon said, "I don't know anyone since Nazi times who has as much Jewish blood on his hands as Arafat."

This is the man who was given the Nobel Peace Prize and whose 1974 UN speech that called for "doing away" with Israel brought a standing ovation.

Israel is not unaware of the kind of treachery that passes for "peace talks" in the Middle East, nor have they forgotten that they enjoyed neither peace nor security when the Arabs held the so-called "West Bank," the Golan Heights, the Gaza, the Sinai Peninsula, and a part of Jerusalem. How will the surrender of that territory now change anything? What is to be gained by embracing another set of hollow promises at the expense of their very survival? How can the thought of a Palestinian state next to Israel not be suicidal when the stated purpose of the Arabs is to acquire sufficient territory to outfit a base for the final assault on the Jewish state?

These are the questions that trouble Ed McAteer, and simply reinforce his commitment to remember what Faye's grandfather told her long ago, to be good to the Jews, citing Genesis 12:1, where the Lord promises to bless those who bless Abraham and his family.

Former mayor of Jerusalem Teddy Kollack is reported to have said, "When Messiah comes, we shall ask, 'Sir, have you been here before?'" Ed believes the Messiah has been here before and he makes no bones about it. And he has no conflict concerning his "witnessing" of his Christian faith to his Jewish friends. "I believe it pleases the Lord," he says, "and that my Savior's love demands it and His smile is upon what we are doing. We're not trying to impose our Christian Scriptures upon anyone. Love doesn't act that way. We are surely living in the 'end of days' and are witnessing the fulfillment of the prophets. Israel is perhaps the greatest witness to this reality.

"The psalmist asks, 'Why do the nations rage and the people imagine a vain thing against the Lord, and against His anointed?' There may be a rage today against this little piece of real estate we call Israel, and against her valiant people, but we know for certain that He Who watches over the 'apple of His eye' neither slumbers nor sleeps, and He will not allow His faithful Word to go unanswered.

"'Come, and let us return to the Lord:
For He has torn, but He will heal us;
He has stricken us, but He will bind us up.
After two days He will revive us;
On the third day He will raise us up,
That we may live in His sight.
Let us know,
Let us pursue the knowledge of the LORD.
His going forth is established as the morning;
He will come to us like the rain.
Like the latter and the former rain to the earth'"
(Hosea 6:1-3).

PROCLAMATION OF BLESSING

As Bible-believing Americans, we believe there exists an ironclad bond between the State of Israel and the United States. We believe that bond to be a moral imperative.

Representing the vast majority of Bible-believing Christians in the United States, we have gathered together at this International Prayer Breakfast to reaffirm our support and prayers that this bond not be weakened or diminished.

As Bible-believing Christians we agree:

"That a secure, strong Israel is in America's self-interest. Israel is a major strategic asset to America. Israel is not a client, but a very reliable friend."

"To weaken Israel is to destabilize the Middle East and risk the peace of the world, for the road to world peace runs through the Middle East."

We support Israel's right to their land spiritually and legally. History records that God deals with nations in accordance with how these nations deal with Israel. We rejoice that here in America, for 228 years, we have been committed to the Jewish people. The Jewish people have found refuge here; they have found a people who love them; and we can take pride in saying that Israel is not an exclusively Jewish issue.

Bible-believing Christians consider the support of Israel a biblical mandate. Regardless of contrary opinion, we do not believe Israel has to offer an excuse for its existence. Israel lives today as a right! A right that has been hallowed by the Bible, by history, by sacrifice, by prayer, and by the yearning for peace.

"I will restore the captivity of my people, Israel…I will plant them in their land, and they will not again be rooted out from their land, which I have given them, says the Lord your God" (Amos 9:14,15).

We believe one of the reasons America has been blessed over the years is because we have stood with Israel. This promise is taken from Genesis 12:3, "I will bless them that bless thee." And so, for biblical reasons first and foremost, we support the State of Israel. For humanitarian reasons, we support the Jewish people. For historical reasons, believing that Palestine belongs to the Jewish people, we support the State of Israel. For legal reasons, dating back to 1948, and even further to the establishment of the British Mandate, we believe the land of Palestine belongs to the Jewish people.

Israel and the United States are not separate and distinct – we are one. We share common ideals and common democracy. What unites us across the ocean, and brings Jew and Christian together, is the recognition that Israel is a nation that is a manifestation of what America was and is.

America has a strong interest in the Middle East. We affirm our belief that the nation of Israel is the key to that interest because of our common bonds, our common values, our common belief in social justice, and the godly principles on which our two countries were founded.

CHAPTER 11

A LOOK AT MORAL ISSUES

Over 1,500 of its 2,200 passengers were lost when the Titanic sank on April 15, 1912, en route to New York from Southampton, on its maiden voyage. Rabbi Daniel Lapin asks an intriguing question in *America's Real War*: "What exact moment condemned the Titanic? Was it the design of the lifeboat systems? Was it the choice of material used in the hull? Was it actually the moment the ship struck the iceberg?" He goes on to say that the sinking of the great ship makes "a perfect metaphor for the expected demise of a great and apparently invulnerable enterprise."

Referring to the United States, he cites some unsettling trends – violence in schools, babies found in dumpsters, assaults on traditional values, rejection of time-honored standards of decency and virtue – then asks, "When did we hit the iceberg?"

Cal Thomas weighs in with an answer: "If you slept through the sixties, you woke to a different America," says the syndicated columnist. "It was the pivotal point of the recent past – an authentic decade of decision. It marked the beginning of a passionate social debate that still divides us. It changed ancient attitudes on matters both public and private." He quotes a sixties' radical who has second thoughts, Peter Collier, who wrote, "The stones we threw into the waters of our world in those days caused ripples that continue to lap on our shores today – for better, and more often, for worse."

"No generation of Americans has ever heard more extravagant promises," says Thomas. "Promises of revolution. Promises of utopia. Promises of ecstasy. Promises of justice." He lists some of the promises made during those days, concluding with *the promise of God's death*. "Few demurred at all when Chicago Seven defendant and militant atheist Abbie Hoffman proclaimed, 'God is dead, and we did it for the kids.'"

Rabbi Lapin concurs with Thomas. Something happened to America in the sixties, but we failed to realize that we had encountered a serious problem. Christian author G.K. Chesterton foretold at the beginning of this century, "Men will more and more realize that there is no meaning in democracy if there is no meaning in anything; and that there is no meaning in anything if the Universe has not a center of significance and an authority that is the author of our rights."

Ed McAteer asserts that the central issue of our time – and of all time – is the existence and sovereignty of God. And flowing from that assertion is the rock-ribbed conviction that there is such a concept as objective truth. There is a bottom line. Life does have meaning and purpose, and to discard that belief is to abandon one's life and one's culture to utter ruin. Social disintegration is inevitable. The frightening thing is that one doesn't wake up some morning to find unpleasant changes inflicted overnight by a foreign invader. We would certainly rise up in righteous revolution were that the case. But that isn't the way a country changes; it happens ever so gradually.

To paraphrase Rabbi Lapin, we have hit an iceberg, but few know it and even fewer care. In the first-class ballroom, the dance continues.

After a grim period, marked by paganism and immorality, eight-year-old Josiah became king of Judea in 640 B.C. He had a heart for God, and early on set about to overturn the disastrous remnants of the evil reigns of his father and his grandfather. In the process of refurbishing the temple, which had fallen into disrepair, Hilkiah, the priest, found a copy of the Law of Moses. He delivered it to King Josiah, who directed that it be read to all the people, which resulted in conviction of sin, revival, and reformation. "And he made all who were in Jerusalem and Benjamin to take a stand" (2 Chronicles 34:32).

Ed McAteer has invested the last thirty years of his life to "taking a stand," raising a standard, sounding the alarm, and rallying the troops. In battling the entrenched evils of our time, he is not unaware of the fact that when standards are discarded and principles are repudiated, the concept of right and wrong becomes a useless relic, an object of scorn. If there is no objective truth, there is no measure by which to make a judgment about anything. "The trouble with us reformers is that we have made reform a crusade against all standards," J. Allen Smith, the father of many modern education reforms, confesses. "Well, we have smashed them all, and now neither we nor anyone else has anything left."

G.K. Chesterton made an amazing statement. "America is the only country in the world that is founded on a creed," he said, "and that creed is set froth with dogmatic and even theological lucidity in the Declaration of Independence."

"Note these words," Ed says, "from the Declaration of Independence: 'We hold these truths to be self-evident...' There is such a thing as absolute truth – unchanging, unchangeable, eternal. Unfortunately, our culture, awash in moral relativism, is blind to it."

To illustrate that, Ed tells of a judge who had to hear a case. When the plaintiff completed his argument, the judge said, "You are right." After the defendant completed telling his side of the story, the judge said, "You are right." A third and impartial counsel spoke up, "Your honor, sir, it cannot be that both sides are right," to which the judge replied, "You, too, are right."

That is relativism, and to embrace it is to sign the death warrant of an individual, a family, a church or synagogue, a nation or a culture.

Christina Hoff Sommers, university professor and author, in an interview with *Christianity Today*, said, "We may be one of the few societies in the world that finds itself incapable of passing on its moral teachings to young people. When it comes to moral teachings to young people, it is as though we've forgotten several thousand years of civilization – the great moral, religious, and philosophical traditions."

Two experiences convinced Sommers that we must find a better way. When she became a parent, she was struck firsthand how public schools retreat from the "traditional task of helping parents to civilize the child." She was grateful to find a private Jewish school where teachers were "not afraid to teach ethics and kindness, where morality was woven into the daily lessons."

What she found in college was equally unsettling. There she encountered a "surprising number of young people who think there's no right or wrong, that moral choices depend on how you feel." They didn't have the slightest idea that morality could be normative and absolute.

Some time ago Sommers published an article titled, "Ethics Without Virtue." She criticized the way ethics is being taught in American colleges. "I pointed out that students taking college ethics classes debate abortion, euthanasia, capital punishment, DNA research, and the ethics of transplant surgery, while they learn almost nothing about private decency, honesty, personal responsibility, or honor." She tells of a colleague who disagreed with her premise. She was focusing on women's oppression, corruption in big business, transgressions of multinational corporations in Third World countries. The colleague explained, "You are not going to have moral people until you have moral institutions. You will not have moral citizens until you have a moral government."

"At the end of the semester," Sommers said, "she came into my office carrying a stack of exams and looking very upset."

"What's wrong?" Sommers asked.

"They cheated on their social justice take-home finals. They plagiarized!" More than half of the students in her ethics class had copied long passages from the secondary literature.

"What are you going to do?" Sommers asked.

"She gave me a self-mocking smile and said, 'I'd like to borrow a copy of that article you wrote on ethics without virtue.'"

Sommers goes on to point out the seriousness of the cheating phenomenon in our schools and universities. "A recent survey reported in the *Boston Globe* says that 50 percent of all college students admit to cheating; for high-school students, the figure is 75 percent. A *U.S. News and World Report* survey asked college-age students if they would steal from an employer. Thirty-four said they would."

What hope does a culture have when it freely discards time-honored truths and traditional values? A *New York Times* editorial writer ridiculed President George W. Bush for being, "intoxicated with moral clarity." Maureen Dowd, the *Times*' gifted but acerbic columnist, commenting on Supreme Court Justice Antonin Scalia, with whose views she dissents, said, "He's so Old School he's Old Testament."

When Ed McAteer reads the *New York Times* Op-ed page, he knows why he founded the Religious Roundtable. "Intoxicated with moral clarity?" McAteer says, "Bring it on!" As for Scalia being so old school he's Old Testament, he doesn't beat around the bush. "If we would have had a little more Old Testament over the last generation, we might now have fewer reporters who fabricate their stories, fewer CEOs who rob the company blind, and fewer accountants who doctor the books." He says, "The price we're paying for wandering in the wilderness of situational ethics is too high."

Ed was a businessman long enough to learn something about the bottom line. Where there is no commitment to objective truth, there is no measure, no scale, no standard, until finally the energy that has fueled a great nation is depleted and the engine stops, the culture dies.

The perceptive Catholic theologian Michael Novak writes, "For it is usually the case that the first generation to reject religion continues to live from the internal capital they have inherited from their belief and its inward practices. However, they have now made themselves incapable of passing on the inner beliefs and practices of their own life to their children. Thus their children grow up in an entirely different situation, and even more so do the children of their children…"

The challenge of passing on these values to the next generation is what energizes Ed McAteer and underscores the importance he places on education. "Our job is to educate," he says, in defining the objective of the Religious Roundtable. "People perish for lack of knowledge. They don't know. They're busy making a living, raising a family, taking care of a thousand necessary things, but are too often unaware of what is happening around them, and the extent to which what is happening will affect their children and their future. So we're in the information business.

"Now to break that down," he continues, "we divide our work into four parts. First, we identify the problem or challenge facing the culture. Then we organize, we get people working together. This is so important. Too often we operate independently and fail to achieve the desired result. Next we go to work explaining what needs to be done. The last step is where it really gets exciting: we direct people into activities that can literally change their communities and their country."

One of Ed's primary concerns is the whole question of abortion, and he believes that people must be educated as to the true nature of this practice if the pro-life cause is to be advanced. He provides a striking example of the importance of this kind of instruction. Ronald Reagan was pro-choice when he was governor of California. But that changed. A Roundtable board member, Dr. Mildred Jefferson, an African-American, Harvard-trained pro-life advocate, spent two hours with

Reagan that changed his mind and set him on a new course. As president, Reagan spoke frequently on the subject and wrote a book about it, the only president to author a book while in the White House. McAteer says he was the most pro-life president we have ever had. When it came to the appointment of Surgeon General, the choice was a strong pro-life advocate, Dr. C. Everett Koop.

Few subjects have evoked more passion. Few issues have stirred more heat in the heart of Ed McAteer, or provoked more action. Dozens of rallies have been held, pamphlets printed, speeches made. Not once, but a thousand times, Ed has articulated his conviction that the primary purpose of government is the protection of human life, and the failure of government to do so is deeply troubling. Keeping the issue before the American people and taking every possible opportunity to combat this evil has been a high priority with this man and his movement.

"Abortion is a contradiction of who we are," says McAteer. "It violates common sense and common decency. It repudiates our character, our history, and our documents, e.g.: "...and are endowed by their Creater with certain unalienable Rights, *among these are Life...*" (italics added). It is a moral outrage unbecoming a nation which for two centuries has championed human rights and welcomed "your tired, your poor, your huddled masses yearning to breathe free." He agrees with Henry Hyde, the Illinois congressman, who has fought the evil of abortion all his public life, who said, "We need prophets and emissaries of transcendence, rather than people who compromise with the world."

If you think Ed McAteer is out on a limb, listen to President Reagan's Surgeon General. In a debate with Dr. Tim Johnson, Dr. Koop said, "Almost no abortions are performed for medical indications; it is expedience that takes most women to the abortionist...because when a pregnant woman decides that she wants an abortion, she is not deciding anything about her health except in rare circumstances. When you say that a woman wants to get rid of something in her body that she has decided will do her more harm than good, you trivialize the abortion issue. That has been the ploy of the pro-abortionists who would like to see abortion taken very lightly as a minor medical issue. That is more than something in her body. It is not, as they say, 'a few membranes in the uterus.' I've never yet asked a woman why she wanted an abortion without getting the answer: I don't want a baby. She knows what it is: a baby. So should society.

"When the abortion debate heated up about twenty-five years ago," Koop continued, "it was primarily social activists and politicians who decided that women should not be 'forced' to undergo an unwanted pregnancy, that a woman has the 'right to her own body,' and that her pregnant plight came about because this is a 'chauvinistic' world. Abortion became a medical issue only because it happened to be doctors who became the executioners of the developing baby. What a travesty for a life-saving profession! When I was a medical student, an abortionist was viewed by the medical profession with a loathing reserved for some slimy crawly thing that came out from under an overturned rock."

These astonishing remarks were not made by a right wing fanatic, but by a highly trained medical doctor who has spent his life healing the sick.

When Dr. Johnson said, "In short, I am morally opposed to abortion but also philosophically opposed to government restriction of free choice and the inevitable discrimination that results," Koop responded, "When you say that you are pro-choice but against abortion, you sound schizophrenic. Tim, I know you wouldn't kill a newborn baby simply because its mother didn't want it. How, then, could you condone taking the life of an unborn baby?

"In Psalm 139, David writes about God's role in his own life before birth: 'For you created my inmost being; you knit me together in my mother's womb. I praise you because I am fearfully and wonderfully made…your eyes saw my unformed body. All the days ordained for me were written in your book before one of them came to be.'

"When God called Jeremiah to be a prophet, we see reference to prenatal purpose in Jeremiah 1:5, 'Before I formed you in the womb, before you were born I set you apart; I appointed you as a prophet to the nations.'"

Ed McAteer has little time for Planned Parenthood of America, whose website directs kids to the internet home of Advocates for Youth, a left-wing Washington, D.C. group where teens can send messages to Congress protesting abstinence-only sex programs and the Bush administration's ban on funding international groups that promote abortion.

Ed refers to the other junior-grade websites that promote abortion and abortion activism to teens. For example, the Coalition for Positive Sexuality (CPS) links abortion and faith in an attempt to convince youth that killing an unborn child is the historical healthcare choice of millions.

"Abortion is a simple medical procedure which ends a pregnancy," the CPS site says. "Throughout history, around the world, and in many religions, women have used abortion as a part of our healthcare…any reason we have for choosing abortion is a good reason."

Albert Mohler, president of Southern Baptist Theological Seminary, says, "America's liberal media are resolutely determined to defend abortion on demand against any threat – no matter how remote. The *New York Times* simply leads the pack in this respect. The *Times* pushes its pro-abortion agenda through slanted news coverage and outright editorial bias. Pro-life leaders are presented as fanatical zealots out to oppress women. Workers in the pro-life movement are portrayed as mindless victims of prejudice and ignorance. The fetus, of course, seldom appears at all."

It was not always so. He quotes Marvin Olasky who demonstrates in *Abortion Rites: A Social History of Abortion in America* that the *New York Times* was once a stalwart defender of human dignity and opposed abortion as "The Great Evil of the Age." "In 1870, editor Louis Jennings published an editorial claiming that the 'perpetration of infant murder' is rank and smells to heaven. Why is there no hint of its punishment? The paper ran a series of investigative reports that led to a police crackdown on abortionists." Mohler suggests, "The current leadership of the *Times* must see this history as a great embarrassment."

Russian lawmakers recently passed the first restrictions on abortion since Joseph Stalin's ban on the procedure was lifted in 1955. While hardly a reversal on abortion policy, it does represent a first step toward the recovery of human life. Predictably, the *New York Times* lamented that "the way may become increasingly dangerous for women if the government arbitrarily curtails medically safe abortions." "Is it not ironic," Ed asks, "that a communist nation seeks to limit the practice of abortion while our God-blessed nation retains the most liberal abortion laws in the Western world?"

When asked to assess the strengths and weaknesses of the conservative movement in dealing with this issue, he speaks candidly. "I think unless we have a real spiritual awakening in America, we are in for trouble. The abortion ruling came along in 1973. I remind people that the wheels of God's justice grind slowly, but they do grind. In 1973, we adopted the concept of the German legal and medical profession of the twenties and thirties: Life is devoid of ultimate value. Under the madman Adolf Hitler, this cheapening of human life reached its nadir in the death camps of Poland and Germany. Isn't there a lesson for us in here somewhere?

"I see a growing commitment to overturn *Roe v. Wade*, more discussion, more awareness about it, and I believe there is a growing concern, but the lifestyle of people today is 'live and let live.' The big thing is getting involved and doing something about it. We send out voter's guides in an attempt to inform people. But we need more pastors in the pulpits to cry out against these things. I say it over and over, people perish for the lack of knowledge. We need to take some practical steps to combat this barbaric practice. We should make it clear that life begins at conception. You don't have to be a Bible thumper to know that. Any intelligent doctor will tell you when life begins. Jesus said, 'I have come that you might have life.' Whatever is second to life is so far back, you cannot see it with a telescope. Again, Jesus said, 'It would be better that a millstone were hanged around your neck rather than offend one of these little ones.' But we're in the wholesale business of offending little ones in this country."

No less troubling to McAteer than the abortion issue is the brazen attempt to legitimize immorality and sexual perversion, assiduously promoted by the media, the entertainment industry, and the educational establishment. The swiftness with which the barriers have come down is stunning. "In 1983, 30 percent of Americans said that they knew someone who was homosexual," write Alan Sears and Craig Osten in *The Homosexual Agenda*, "By 2000, that figure had skyrocketed to 73 percent. In 1985, only 40 percent of those polled said they were comfortable around individuals who practice homosexual behavior. By 2000, that figure has risen to 60 percent. Also in 1985, 90 percent of Americans said they would be upset if their son or daughter announced they were homosexual. By 2000, that figure stood at just 37 percent. How has 1 and 2 percent of the population achieved so much success in transforming American culture and restricting religious freedom?"

They quote Gene Edward Veith, who wrote about the gains made by the homosexual activist movement: "Homosexuality used to be considered a vice; now even those it makes uncomfortable must avow – as in a Seinfeld episode – 'not that there's anything wrong with it,' while those who think there is something wrong with it are considered to have the vice of intolerance."

How do you account for such a radical shift in public attitudes and how did it occur in less than one generation? The well-thought-out strategy, devised in part by activists Marshall Kirk and Hunter Madsen, was publicized in a 1987 article titled, *The Overhauling of Straight America* and a 1989 book titled *After the Ball.* They lay out a six-point strategy to change America's perception of homosexual behavior:

1. Talk about gays and gayness as loudly and often as possible.
2 Portray gays as victims, not aggressive challengers.
3 Give homosexual protectors a "just" cause.
4 Make gays look good.
5. Make the victimizers look bad.
6. Solicit funds: the buck stops here (i.e., get corporate America and major corporations to financially support the cause).

Kirk and Madsen write, "The principle behind this advice is simple: almost all behavior begins to look normal if you are exposed to enough of it at close quarters and among your acquaintances."

Speakers at the 1999 Gay, Lesbian, Straight Educational Network (GILSEN), in outlining their agenda, made no attempt to camouflage their true intentions: "The fear of the religious right is that the schools of today will be the government of tomorrow. And you know, they're right. If we do our jobs right, we're going to raise a generation of kids who don't believe the claims of the religious right."

Ed McAteer cites Genesis 19 and asserts that the very future of our nation is at stake. He sounds like a prophet when he opens the Bible and reads from Hosea 4:6: "My people are destroyed for lack of knowledge. Because you have rejected knowledge, I also will reject you from being priest for Me; because you have forgotten the law of your God, I also will forget your children."

"It is our children who are in the cross hairs," Ed warns. "They are being targeted every day of their lives."

Sears and Osten declare that the National Education Association (NEA) is more than a willing partner in this debasement of our culture. "While the NEA has been promoting the homosexual agenda for years," they write, "its most blatant attempt was at its 2001 annual convention in Los Angeles. At that convention, the NEA considered a resolution to implement promotion of full-scale indoctrination of children to accept and affirm homosexual behavior. The resolution read as follows:

"'The National Education Association recognizes the complex and diverse needs of gay, lesbian, bisexual, transgender, and questioning students; and gay, lesbian, bisexual, and transgender families and their children require the development of programs to promote a safe and inclusive environment.'"

They list the steps designed to achieve a "safe and inclusive environment." They include development of curriculum and instructional materials and programs designed to meet the needs of gay and lesbian students, involvement of gay and lesbian characters in material used in the classroom, and recognition of the importance of gay, lesbian, bisexual, and transgender education employees as role models, among other things.

The resolution could have disastrous consequences for an entire generation of children. Though implementation of the resolution was "tabled" for further "study" following criticism from groups such as Focus on the Family, NEA president Bob Chase says, "Let me make it clear…in no way is the NEA backing down from the important issues raised by this resolution…Some critics want the public schools to be an agent of moral doctrine, condemning children and adults when they are not in accord with Biblical principles."

"Think about that statement for a second," Sears and Osten warn. "The NEA is condemning parents who object to homosexual behavior and believe that it should not be taught in public schools, accusing them of forcing their 'moral doctrine' on children. It is not by coincidence that the very first thing that God created after the heavens and the earth was the family. It is his institution for the raising and nurturing of children. If we wreck what God has ordained, the generations that follow will reap the consequences of our action."

Is America at the crossroads, or did we long ago pass that juncture, make a bad choice, and are we now heading in the wrong direction? Have we collided with an iceberg, but don't know it? Are the waters even now rushing into the watertight compartments down below? If so, why does the dancing continue in the first-class ballroom?

The men of Israel trembled at the sight of Goliath and were terrorized by his threats, when a shepherd boy pushed his way past armored vehicles, privates and generals, peered at the giant across the valley, and asked, "Is there not a cause? Is not our God able to help us?" Then he picked up five smooth stones and loaded his slingshot.

Thirty years ago, a toothpaste salesman, alarmed by the near-universal rejection of truth, the shameless disregard for human life, and the giddy clamoring for "strange sins and startling obscenities," made a decision that led him from the boardroom to the battlefield. When asked why he walked away from success and security to engage in a relentless battle against great odds, he bristles. "Is there not a cause?" he asks. "Are not the weapons of our warfare mighty through God? Shall the Lord's name be reproached and His people remain silent? Is there not a man among us who will stand in the gap?"

Ed McAteer pauses under the weight of these questions – then looks for five smooth stones.

CHAPTER 12

LOOKING AHEAD

During the Reagan administration, before a newly appointed diplomat departed for a tour of duty, Secretary of State George Schultz would invite him to his office, lead him to a large globe, spin it around, and say, "Now show me your country." After the diplomat pointed to his assigned destination, Schultz would locate the United States, put his finger on it and say, "*This* is your country."

Ed McAteer has an ongoing love affair with this country, this unique, exceptional and God-blessed nation. He remembers it as it once was, to quote Andree Seu, senior writer for WORLD magazine, "…before *Roe v. Wade* in 1973, the same year the American Psychiatric Association declassified homosexuality as an illness…It was before Chili's eatery ran an ad showing a de-closeted gay athlete, and lesbian couples were enlisted to sell Volvos. It was before "Boy Meets Boy' went from fringe to family fare. It was before the Episcopal church not only accepted homosexuality but gave it the bishop's mitre, and before Massachusetts' highest court made ready to consider the legality of gay unions."

Ed fears that we may have thrown overboard the moral compass which guided us for two hundred years, and are now sailing by dead reckoning. He is certain that our very survival depends upon the participation of virtuous people. The Founding Fathers were convinced that no country could remain free unless virtuous, and virtue could not exist in the absence of faith. Therefore, people of faith must stand up and be counted if the growing tide of secularism is to be stemmed before it is too late.

Natan Sharansky, a Soviet dissident who spent nine years in the Soviet prison system, much of it in solitary confinement, is now a minister in the Israeli government. In *Fear No Evil*, he tells how Bibles brought to Russia by tourists shed light on their bleak existence. Reading the Hebrew Scriptures, they learned that Jews had years of history. They were part of an unfolding drama; they were not alone, and Sharansky made a profound discovery, one that would sustain him through years of deprivation, punishment and pain. "The minute you have an identity," he said, "you are a free person."

Identity and freedom are indissoluble. Before a people can be enslaved, they must be anesthetized. Memory must be destroyed, history overturned. Said Solzhenitzen, "To destroy a people you must first sever their roots." The Killing Fields of Cambodia were impossible until the intelligentsia, the professionals, the teachers and ministers, were dispensed with. The gods are dethroned and the temples desecrated because dictators cannot abide dissent.

"If we forget what we did, we won't know who we are," said Ronald Reagan in his farewell address to the American people. "I am warning of the eradication of...the American memory, that could result, ultimately, in erosion of the American spirit."

Balint Vazsonyi, Hungarian-born historian and world renowned concert pianist, writes in *American's 30 Years War*, "The elimination of the nation's true history, expertly practiced in the Soviet Union and the Third Reich, guarantees commissars an uncontested field as they bring generations with blanks instead of history in their heads. Those blank areas can be filled with anything the commissars invent. There are no beacons of the past, no common orientation, no grid of references to contradict the propaganda. That is why America's founding documents have been removed from the classroom. That is why civics classes have disappeared along with George Washington's birthday. History is the national memory. No history – no national memory – no identity.

According to the Italian Communist Antonio Gramsci, if a revolution is to succeed, "we must first de-Christianize the West." The culture must be changed, he insisted; to do so requires a "long march through the institutions" – the church, the schools and universities, the media.

In *The Greening of America*, Charles Reich explains the process: "There is a revolution coming. It will not be like revolutions of the past. It will originate with the individual and the culture, and it will change the political structure only as its final act. It will not require violence to succeed, and it cannot be successfully resisted with violence. It is now spreading with amazing rapidity, and already our laws, institutions and social structure are changing in consequence."

"This is your country," George Schultz declared. To love it, support and defend it, McAteer will tell you, is not to suggest that the flag waves over utopia or that paradise has arrived. He recalls a visit with Jesse Jackson. "I'm pretty outspoken," Ed admits, "especially with people I like. I bumped into the colorful, civil rights activist some time ago, and I said, "Jesse, you're supposed to be a preacher, and you've spent your life running around trying to cause trouble. Why do you do that?"

"Let me tell you something, Ed," Jackson replied, "when I was nine years old, my daddy was a janitor in a white Baptist church, and on Sunday morning I had to stay outside. I heard the singing and wanted to go in." "Hold it right there," McAteer cut in, "if I had a million tongues, I couldn't tell you how wrong that is. That you were prevented from attending a worship service in any church was a disgrace. But all of us have experienced some misfortune in our lives. I was an orphan. I didn't have a mother or a father. I could be bitter about life, too. But I rejoice in it. I've learned things through the difficulties I wouldn't otherwise have known. But to capitalize on your bitterness is not right. He said, 'Ed, I'd like to talk to you some more,' and he gave me his private home phone number. I consider him a good friend."

McAteer adds, "This country is the last best hope for humanity, and our distinctive American values are worth fighting and dying for, but I'm not impervious to the nation's ills. Take the scandalous assault on the Boy Scouts. The 1911 Scout handbook declares 'no boy can grow into the best kind of citizen without recognizing an obligation to God.' Until recently, no one had a problem with the Scouts' acknowledgment of God or with their stand for moral purity. Now, to the *New York Times*, the Boy Scouts are 'something akin to a hate group.' Numerous United Way chapters as well as large corporations have lifted support, and municipalities have withdrawn support and restricted their use of public facilities."

When the Eagle Scouts participated in opening ceremonies at the Democratic convention in Los Angeles, the delegates booed. Wrote reporter Valerie Richardson: "Under normal circumstances, jeering at children is the sort of behavior that might get a delegate sanctioned, if not booted from the convention altogether. But anyone who expected the Democratic leadership to scold the Boy Scouts of America bashers is attending the wrong convention." (Contrast the wild applause accorded the Des Moines Gay Men's Choir at the Iowa Democratic convention).

The practice of abortion is a stain on our national soul. On one floor of the hospital babies are delivered, and on another floor babies are killed. That is a stark and chilling statement, but it is accurate, and no euphemism can make something ugly appear beautiful. It would take six hundred Viet Nam Memorial Walls to list all the nameless human persons who have perished at the hands of doctors who have forgotten their Hippocratic Oath.

Dr. Bernard Nathanson, author of *The Hand of God*, had seventy three thousand encounters with the grisly procedure. He aborted his own child, and the unborn children of friends, colleagues, and casual acquaintances, even teachers. When ultra-sound opened up a new world, enabling doctors and parents to "really see the human fetus, measure it, watch it, and indeed bond with it, he wrote an article in the *New England Journal of Medicine* expressing doubts about the morality of abortion. He was inundated with stacks of mail and overwhelmed by the vituperation and threats it contained. "Abortion is a crime," he concludes.

Then you have presidential aspirant Wesley Clark, who told the Manchester (N.H.) Union Leader, "Life begins with the mother's decision." Writing in WORLD magazine, Gene Edward Veith says, "The assumption is that there are no objective moral criteria that apply to abortion. If a woman chooses to have a baby, that's right 'for her.' If she chooses to have an abortion, that is right for her. What makes something right is the act of choice."

One wonders where the insanity stops, and recalls something Richard Weaver wrote in *Ideas Have Consequences* in 1947, "There are grounds for declaring that modern man has become a moral idiot."

Ed McAteer tirelessly insists that the first business of government is the protection life, and government's failure to protect life, like the blood on Lady McBeth's hands, is a stain that will not go away. One can almost hear an old prophet leveling a solemn charge: "The sin of Judah is written with a pen of iron; with the point of a diamond it is engraved on the tablet of their heart, and on the horns of your altars" (Jeremiah 17:1).

Then there is the strange and growing threat posed by the homosexual agenda, poised to engulf the entire culture, aided and abetted by willing accomplices in the media, the world of entertainment and the education establishment. The

New York Times national political correspondent Richard Berke told colleagues at the tenth anniversary reception of the National Lesbian and Gay Journalists Association, "Three quarters of the people who decide what goes on the front page (of the *Times*) are 'not-so-closeted' homosexuals." The resulting bias explains why the health hazard related to moral perversion is covered up. *Psychological Reports* said in a 1998 article that 'the average life expectancy of homosexuals is 20 to 30 years less than heterosexuals. Why then do we promote such a life style?

And this tinkering with the meaning of marriage! Liberal columnist Michael Kinsley wrote a piece in the *Washington Post* titled, "Abolish Marriage; Let's Really Get Government out of Our Bedrooms." He writes, "The solution is to end the institution of marriage, or rather, the solution is to end the institution of government monopoly on marriage. And yes, if three people want to get married, or one person wants to marry herself, and someone else wants to conduct a ceremony and declare them married, let 'em. If you and your government aren't implicated, what do you care? If marriage were an entirely private affair, all the disputes over gay marriages would become irrelevant."

Dr. James Dobson is not amused. "Polygamy, anyone?" he asks. "That is precisely what the more radical activists want. And as we all know, they have gotten nearly everything they have cooked up in recent years.

"Admittedly, this hostility to marriage is not all that new. In 1918, Russian revolutionary Vladimir Lenin abolished marriage and declared the family obsolete. His motive was simple: the 'family' prevented women from doing work that was useful to the state. Do you see the stunning parallel to the current crisis of our times? The stability of the American family today is not only being slandered, but slaughtered! Indeed, bad things will continue to happen if good people do nothing."

A state governor recently said, "When it comes to social issues, I'm not all one way or the other." Have we lost our ability to make judgments based on fixed moral law? Have we made a covenant with death? Have we abandoned all semblance of sanity? Are "the timbers of the old house rotting"? Cyril Connally wrote a half century ago, "It is closing time in the gardens of the West."

Ed McAteer is not blind to the nation's ills, neither is he despairing. He is quite settled on the fact that God is not dead nor does He sleep. There are battles to be fought and victories won, and he's not discouraged. He believes God has called him to "blow the alarm in Zion," and rally the people for the fight of their lives to recapture the culture. If victory were not possible, God would not have called us, so this is no time to forsake the struggle. In *When Nations Die*, Jim Nelson Black nails the Evangelicals: "But one of the greatest reasons for the decline of American society over the past century has been the tendency of Christians who have practical solutions to abandon the forum at the first sign of resistance. Evangelicals in particular have been quick to run and slow to stand by their beliefs. In reality, most Christians had already vacated 'the public square' of moral and political debate by their own free will, long before civil libertarians and others came forth to drive us back to our churches."

"Victory is never final and defeat is never fatal," said Britain's wartime Prime Minister Winston Churchill. Ed McAteer knows something of both, so he is neither unduly elated when good things happen nor sorely depressed when things turn out badly. One of the challenges he wrestles with is the tendency of "the establishment" to forget promises made during an election once victory is declared. In 1980, Ed almost single-handedly rounded up thousands of preachers for the historic National Affairs Briefing in Dallas. So successful was the meeting that Morton Blackwell, then chief White House liaison to the Evangelical right, called it "a major turning point in the history of the United States."

"One would think that the victors owed a debt of gratitude to McAteer and his warriors," writes S.R. Shearer, radio commentator and author. "But when the time came to collect on his debt in his 1984 run for the Republican nomination for the seat vacated by Senator Howard Baker of Tennessee, he was unceremoniously shoved aside by party leaders in favor of an old-line GOP regular. Many old-line Republicans were more than a little embarrassed by McAteer's fervent embrace of some of the Evangelical's social agenda and the aura of "red-neck fundamentalism" which some felt surrounded him. They even prevailed upon many of Ed's erstwhile friends to abandon him in favor of someone more acceptable to them. McAteer was abandoned by the party and left dangling in the wind.

"It seems that Evangelicals are welcomed into the kitchen via the back door," Shearer added, "but they are not welcomed into the living room where the real party is going on."

It is safe to say that Ronald Reagan was one of the most beloved presidents in recent American history. He did more to advance the conservative cause than anyone in the last century. But in some ways, those issues considered by conservatives to be non-negotiable were scarcely advanced at all. Even now, after some disastrous United States Supreme Court decisions, it is painful to note that the decision nullifying the Texas anti-sodomy law "was read by a former appointee of Ronald Reagan, and four of the six on the majority side were appointed by Republicans."

Shearer recounts the struggle to have Evangelicals appointed in the Bush administration following Ronald Reagan. "The personnel selection process got off to a rocky start, he remembers. "Judge Paul Pressler of Houston, a conservative lay leader in the Southern Baptist Convention and a longtime friend of George Bush, was originally recommended for Solicitor General or federal district judge. He later accepted the newly created post of ethics czar, but withdrew his name from consideration after he came under attack from liberal Baptists and moderates within the Bush White House, who leaked allegations against him to the *Washington Post*. The pattern repeated itself numerous times. Pro-family leaders also lobbied for Patricia Heinz, who had served in the Reagan

White House, for a slot as Assistant Secretary of Education, a powerful post with oversight over much of the educational budget. When Senator Ted Kennedy objected, Heinz instead received a post at the Pentagon overseeing the training of Navy personnel, a job that did not require Senate confirmation. Another strong conservative, Hal Ezell, was serving as a deputy regional commissioner of the Immigration and Naturalization Service. Evangelicals concerned with Jewish emigration from the Soviet Union wanted him reappointed, but he was dumped in favor of a party loyalist.

"In the end, few evangelicals were appointed, or, for that matter, carried over from the Reagan years. By the time the Bush administration held its first cattle call for religious leaders in November 1989, the grumbling was becoming clearly audible. In what was supposed to be a typical handholding exhibition at the White House, several rose to challenge Chase Untemeyer, director of presidential personnel, as to why so few evangelicals had been selected for prominent posts. Untemeyer argued that it violated the law to "count" people according to their religious beliefs.

"Finally, Pat Robertson rose to speak. 'Isn't it interesting that you have no difficulty identifying evangelicals and their allies during the campaign,' he said, 'but you cannot find them after the election.' The room exploded with laughter and applause."

In the seventh decade of his life, Ed McAteer finds himself in the thick of the battle. It is at times challenging, sometimes exhilarating, but never boring. He is incorrigibly cheerful. He can't help it. The joy of the Lord is his strength. He is like a tree planted by the rivers of water. God is his rock and his defense, for after all, the battle is the Lord's. He often quotes George Washington, who, upon being elected president of the Constitutional Convention in 1787, said, "Let us raise a standard to which the wise and honest can repair; the event is in the hands of God."

Ed McAteer is raising a standard. The events are in the hands of God.

CHAPTER 13

PROFILE OF A PATRIOT

A patriot is defined as a person who loves, supports, and defends his or her country and its interest with devotion. "If I had a vein which did not beat with the love of my country, I would open it," said Gen. Pinckney, one of the delegates to the Constitutional Convention in 1787.

Euripides wrote, "There is no greater sorrow on earth, than the loss of one's native land."

It was that sense of loss that drove Ed McAteer to make a radical decision in mid-life. This orphan boy, who rose to fabled success in the corporate world, saw his country slipping away and resolved to do something about it. He abandoned an executive position with a multi-billion dollar company and enlisted in the Lord's army. He's been sounding the alarm and rallying the troops ever since.

"Why not stay a little longer?" a friend reasoned. "Don't give up your career and retirement." But McAteer would not be deterred. He had taken a long look down the road and what he saw hardened his resolve- the removal of prayer and Bible reading from the schools; the dismantling of the Judeo-

Christian framework which had served so well for 200 years, and the chiseling away at our prized liberties, and the brazen assault on Constitutional principles and Biblical values.

What was most troubling was that too few good people seemed to notice. Life wasn't all that bad in this good land thirty-five years ago, but what of the future? Were we living beyond our means? Were we tapping into borrowed capital, enjoying the benefits of our fathers' labors without replenishing the store? Will there be anything left in the bank when our children are ready to do business? How long can a people squander their moral resources until they are forced into receivership?

Two new cars in the garage, a handsome salary, security, pension and perks – but the nagging questions wouldn't go away.

Whatever happened to America? By what circuitous route did we become a nation adrift, beset by violence in our homes, in our schools, and on our streets? How did a once proud nation now find itself reeling beneath the weight of drug addiction, teenage pregnancies, crime, dysfunctional families, private debt and public debt?

Maybe it's time to dust off the old prophets and listen to their solemn warning, McAteer thought. Isaiah lived in a time not unlike ours, when people had forgotten God. "The ox knows its owner and the donkey its master's crib," Isaiah cried, "but Israel does not consider…they have forsaken the Lord and they have provoked to anger the Holy One of Israel, they have turned away backward" (Isa. 1:3, 4).

Jeremiah witnessed the physical destruction of the city of Jerusalem when Nebuchadnezzar and his armies, on three different incursions, invaded Judah, taking many of its inhabitants captive to Babylon. The prophet remained in the city and witnessed firsthand homes being burned to the ground, the women ravished, the young men murdered, the glorious temple ransacked and looted. "Is it nothing to you, all you who pass by?" Jeremiah asks. "Behold and see if there is any sorrow like my sorrow which has been brought upon me" (Lam. 1:12). As

God dealt with Israel long ago, he deals with nations today. The tragedy today, as then, is that too few seem to care.

And where are the Lord's people? Is there not a cause? McAteer would agree with theologian R.C. Sproul, who recently wrote, "I doubt if there has been a period in all of Christian history when so many Christians are so ineffectual in shaping the culture in which they live as is true right now."

The failure of evangelical believers to share their faith in the marketplace of ideas and participate in public life has left a vacuum to be filled by others whose agenda is inimical to the best interests of our country.

A stark example of such a failure is found in the history of Germany in the late thirties and forties. The once-proud nation lay prostrate following defeat in the First World War and the humiliating "terms of peace" imposed at Versailles. Hitler years before had mapped out a strategy for German conquest. It was spelled out in great detail in *Mein Kamph*, written while incarcerated at Lansberg prison. Now ensconced in the chancellorship, he was ready to implement those plans. But he had a big problem.

Germany was the most religious country in Europe. Hitler respected and feared the church and knew he could not achieve his aims so long as there was one competing voice. He must be the single authority. Therefore the church must be silenced or subdued – or compromised.

Compromise became the strategy.

Hitler summoned the leading clergymen to the Reichstag – the parliament building in Berlin. He outlined his plans to lift the nation out of the ashes and shed the memory of defeat. Germany will rise again, he promised. He complimented the pastors and solicited their support, then threw out the bait: "You preachers take care of the churches," he said, "and I will take care of Germany."

Who could argue with that? It's the same mantra we have heard in this country for two generations: Worship God if you wish, but do it privately. Sing your anthems in church and read the Bible in your homes, but don't let its precepts color your thinking or influence your behavior in the workplace or on the campus. Do not allow traditional beliefs, standards of decency and virtue to shape the culture. Let the politicians and educators do that.

Hitler will take care of the state.

Not a murmur of protest arose in the Reichstag that day until one Lutheran pastor stood, walked to the dais, and said, "Herr Hitler, Jesus Christ will take care of His churches. I'm concerned about Germany's soul."

He soon found himself in jail. When the chaplain came by the next morning, he was surprised to see the prominent pastor behind bars. "Brother Martin, why are you in here?" To which Niemoller responded, "Brother, given the situation in our country, why aren't you in here?"

Dietrich Bonhoeffer, who was hanged at Flossenburg prison a month before the war ended had protested, saying that the church should "jam the spokes of the wheel of the state if the persecution of the Jews should continue."

Martin Niemoller never forgot the price his countrymen paid for the failure of the churches to "jam the spokes" in Germany's darkest hour. In later years, he often concluded a speech with these now familiar lines:

They came for the Communists,
and I didn't object – for I was not a Communist.
They came for the socialists, and I didn't object
because I was not a socialist.
They then came for the labor leaders,
and I didn't object because I was not a labor leader.
They came for the Jews, and I didn't object
because I was not a Jew.
Then they came for me, and
There was no one left to object.

Helen Kromer in the musical review of *For Heaven Sake*,

has caught the thrust of this thought in her chorus, "One Man Awake":

One man awake can awaken another.
The second can waken his next door brother
The three awake can rouse a town
By turning the whole place upside down!
The many awake can make such a fuss
That it finally awakens the rest of us,
One man up with dawn in his eyes, multiplies.

"One man up with dawn in his eyes," is a perfect example of Ed McAteer. And, he believes you don't have to be mean-spirited to bring about positive change. Many religious and community leaders were troubled a number of years ago when 7-Eleven stores introduced a wide range of magazines and tabloids, which they considered to be pornographic. Because children and young people frequented these stores, a petition was circulated to protest the decision made by the Southland Corporation which owned the 7-Eleven stores. When McAteer's signature on the petition was sought, he said, "Give me a little time."

The president of Southland Corporation had given $50,000 toward the half million- dollar budget of the National Affairs Briefing in Dallas. Ed McAteer is not for sale, but he is a gentleman, so he made an appointment with the president. "A good many people are not happy with your decision to bring a certain type of magazines to your stores. We don't think it's in the best interest of the community and we don't think it's in your best interest. A petition is being circulated to express these feelings, which I will sign if necessary. But I wanted to talk to you first, because I know you love this country as much as I do."

"My wife is very outspoken about this," the president said. "She's not too happy with what we're doing. Thank you, Ed for bring this to my attention." Within two weeks, the magazines disappeared from the 7-Eleven stores.

Harriet Beecher Stowe was married to a preacher and teacher and raised a brood of children. Later she took to writing, and after some success as an author, her sister-in-law in Boston wrote to her saying, "Hattie, if I could use the pen as you can, I would write something that will make this whole nation feel what an accursed thing slavery is."

Harriet's husband, Calvin, thought little of the book. Her publisher was unimpressed, but the people loved it. "Within a week after publication," best-selling author David McCullough relates, "ten thousand copies had been sold. The publisher had three presses running 24 hours a day. In a single year, sales in the United States came to more than 300,000."

The book made publishing history right from the start. In England, where Mrs. Stowe had no copyright and therefore received no royalties, sales were even more stupendous. A million and a half copies were sold in about a year's time. The book appeared in 37 languages. "It is no longer permissible to those who can read not to have read it," wrote George Sand from France, who called the author a saint who had no talent, only genius.

The book was *Uncle Tom's Cabin*. Lincoln is supposed to have said as he shook Stowe's hand, "So this is the little woman who made this big war."

Uncle Tom's Cabin became a catalyst in outlawing slavery in the United States.

"No one thought the young man standing in front of a tank in Tiananmen Square, would be successful in deterring the Chinese army from firing its appointed rounds," Cal Thomas writes, "but that image spoke to a world gone mushy about the power of one. Statuary Hall in the U.S. Capitol is lined with marble memorials to men and women of courage who stood against what was popular, and upheld what was right and virtuous. America's Founders risked their lives and fortunes, but because they stood for principle against seemingly impossible odds, none lost his honor."

Because McAteer stood on principle, sometimes against seemingly impossible odds, he didn't lose his honor – and he never lost heart. Undaunted by hard work, hectic schedules, incessant travel, betrayal and disappointment, he never looked back. There were stunning successes and crushing defeats, but no slackening of pace.

A seasoned warrior doesn't fight battles that aren't worth winning. By the same token, he may engage the conflict when the outcome is not altogether certain. Compromise may be the art of politics, but when it comes to moral issues, the "art of politics" doesn't appeal to McAteer. When it comes to choosing the lesser of two evils, he's not in the market. Any degree of evil is to be resisted.

When he learned that Sandra Day O'Connor might be appointed to the Supreme Court, wary of her stand on abortion, he went into action. "Don't embarrass the administration," friends argued. Instead of being persuaded, he marshaled the troops, held press conferences and organized rallies. Ed McAteer has a gracious way about him, but he is not soft. When it comes to the abortion issue, he is adamant. He considers the slaughter of innocents a national disgrace, and his passion is that of a Baptist evangelist when he discusses it. He will remind you that one of the few stated purposes of government is to protect human life, and its failure to do so is nothing short of scandalous.

This man who walked away from everything he had worked for for twenty-five years saw no merit in selling out for political correctness at this juncture in his life. There was the time he announced his candidacy for the United States Senate. When his decision didn't fit the scheme of the power brokers, he was offered a prize if he would reconsider: A position in the White House with generous salary and a quarter-of-a-million dollar budget for staff – and more if needed. No deal. Some issues are simply non-negotiable, like his unflagging support for the State of Israel. This is "a hill worth fighting for," and he will not be deterred. His inflexible position is expressed in biblical language: "If I forget thee, O Jerusalem, let my tongue cleave to the roof of my mouth."

Paul Weyrich, chairman and CEO of Free Congress Foundation, says, "What I keep trying to convince the secular-humanist politicians is that in dealing with an Ed McAteer they're dealing with someone beyond the ordinary. Ed and those working with him and responding to him are not moved by the ordinary temporal considerations that concern modern man. As a consequence, this segment of the movement is much more likely to adhere to principle than some of the others."

Ed McAteer is cut from the same cloth as Oklahoma's Dr. Tom Coburn, who made – and kept – a promise that if elected to Congress he would serve three terms and return home. This is the man who said, "Every politician should get up in the morning prepared to make a decision that will end his career."

A man of character keeps his word and is not ready for the day until he has buckled on the belt of truth. President Reagan once said, "We made quite a stir when everybody found out that we were going to do just what we said we were going to do."

McAteer identifies with that sentiment and scoffs at the suggestion of a former Washington, D.C. mayor: "There are two kinds of truth – real truth and made-up truth."

When it comes to honesty, integrity, truthfulness, McAteer's advice is simple, "Buy the truth and sell it not" – and never leave home without it.

A clear vision, sound thinking, devotion to one's country, adherence to principle, an unwillingness to quit, and unquestioned integrity. This is the profile of a patriot. This is the story of Ed McAteer – but it's only part of the story.

If he has a love affair with his country, he has a passion for Jesus Christ. "God and country" is not a cliché, it is an indissoluble bond – and "blessed is that nation whose God is the Lord."

This former marketing executive is a Christian first, a citizen second, and his Christian faith both transcends and undergirds every aspect of his public life. Because access to heaven is more important than access to the White House, the shaping of legislation or winning elections, prayer becomes the breath of his soul. His day begins and ends with it and the walls of his office and home are mute testimony to its constant practice.

His faith rubs off on every relationship. When a grandson comes in there is a show of affection, a look of pride, some words of encouragement and a brief prayer before he leaves. His romance with Faye has lasted fifty-five years. It is the glue that holds the family together. His home is a haven, his marriage a model, and his children and grandchildren rise up and call him blessed.

His office walls are lined with mementoes, newspaper stories, certificates of appreciation, framed letters, honorary degrees and pictures. Ronald Reagan is there as are the Bushes and Ariel Sharon. Howard Phillips, Benjamin Netanyahu, John Ashcroft, Charles Stanley, Adrian Rogers, Jack Kemp, Bob Dole, Jerry Falwell, Paul Weyrich, and Phyllis Schlafley. It's a walk-through of history with generals and statesmen, as well as plain folk; a veritable gallery of Who's Who in the conservative movement, friends and colleagues who articulated the issues, took up the battles and fought in the trenches.

He is no stranger to the Oval Office, having served five presidents or presidential candidates. He has traveled the world, was arrested in Colombia for witnessing, and flew with the first planeload of Russian Jews en route to Israel. He has been a witness to history and has made history, and was once listed among the hundred most influential people in America.

But at the end of the day, only a few things matter, things like faith, family, and freedom. Defining and defending them remain his passion, passing them on to the next generation, his mission.

"The reason I stay in the battle," McAteer says, "is because anything is possible with God. It makes no difference whether He saves by few or by many. When Gideon started his battle, he had 32,000 men, but God brought him down to 300.

So we can never tell – we have to have some guidelines, benchmarks, but as long as we have breath in our bodies and know what's right, and we have the freedom to speak out and organize, we'll keep going. It's always too soon to quit."

Someone suggested the former soap salesman and amateur boxer may be slowing up. Don't count on it. As long as there is an opponent in the ring, don't look for E.E. "Ed" McAteer to hang up the gloves.

APPENDIX A

THE ROUNDTABLE'S POSITION ON CONTROVERSIAL ISSUES

The following position statement is printed as an aid to the reader in formulating a basis from which to discuss, debate and defend a biblically-consistent position on controversial issues of today.

CHURCH AND STATE

It is clear in the U.S. Constitution that the church is not to dominate the state and the state is not to dominate the church. The famous First Amendment declares that "Congress shall make no law respecting an establishment of religion, or prohibiting the free exercise thereof."

The Roundtable is committed irrevocably to this constitutional principle. The American idea from the beginning was liberation from the "state church" tyranny of the old world, which so frequently persecuted those who, for reasons of faith and conscience, refused to conform.

CHRISTIAN POLITICAL ACTIVISM

The false propaganda that the separation of church and state means the separation of God and Christians from state has been partly responsible for the spiritual, moral and governmental decline that has occurred in recent decades.

In a Republic such as ours, every Christian represents a unit of political influence. Failure to exercise that unit of influence on behalf of godly principles always paves the way for the rule of the godless, which is clearly contrary to God's will for any nation (Psalm 125:3).

The political process is the main mechanism for leadership selection – and biblical history demonstrates that the fortunes of a nation are directly related to the spiritual-moral quality of its leadership.

PRAYER IN SCHOOLS

The Roundtable advocates voluntary prayer in tax-supported schools, with adherents of each faith allowed to meet, read scriptures and pray freely in a non-coercive environment. This is no more a violation of church-state separation than are the opening of Supreme Court sessions or the U.S. Senate with prayer.

In fact, the Roundtable believes the *prohibition* of voluntary prayer in schools is a violation of the "free exercise" clause of the First Amendment. Surely if religion may be exercised freely, it should neither be barred from nor imposed upon any forum or institution in the nation. The military establishment is tax-supported, yet the provision of chaplaincy service has never been regarded as a violation of the doctrine of church-state separation.

"The Lord has a controversy with the inhabitants of the land, because there is no truth, nor mercy, nor knowledge of God in the land" (Hosea 4:1).

ABORTION

Human life begins at the moment of fertilization. The fetus is just as human as is an adult person. The deliberate killing of the human fetus, at any stage of development, is a brutal act of murder.

The judgment of God will surely fall on a nation which allows the mass murder of millions of pre-born human beings. For this horrible sin America must reckon with the holy and just God of the universe. Every godly citizen should use his influence to help put a stop to this pervasive curse in our society.

HOMOSEXUAL RIGHTS

No special rights should be extended to homosexuals on the basis of their homosexual identity. Homosexual practices can bring the wrath of God upon a people, as dramatized by the destruction of Sodom. America must not legitimize this monstrous sin by yielding to the demands of those who demonstrate for special "rights" on the basis of it.

WOMEN'S LIBERATION

The radical so-called "liberationist" movements among women today are for the most part anti-God, immoral and degrading to womanhood. The ERA would remove the distinctions between male and female, thus opening the door to homosexual marriages, single-sex families, the drafting of women into the military services for combat duty, and a host of other evils.

Historically, only the Gospel has elevated women from the drudgery and slavery that was their lot in the ancient world. Spiritual liberation is the only effective basis of political liberation.

"He that justifieth the wicked, and he that condemneth the just, even they both are abomination to the Lord." (*Proverbs 17:15*)

WELFARE

The Bible is clear in its declaration that God will judge government leaders for injustice toward orphans and widows (Isaiah 1:23), for spoiling or robbing the poor (Isaiah 3:14) and for grinding the faces of the poor (Isaiah 3:15). On the other hand, the Bible nowhere justifies the use of coercive government power to plunder some elements of society and dole out to others.

The socialist welfare state de-motivates the productive people by robbing them in the name of doing good, and at the same time dehumanizes and destroys the unproductive people by encouraging dependency. Welfare belongs to the church and the private sector. The secular welfare state mentality is a curse which has helped bring America to the brink of economic calamity. It must be counteracted and stopped.

CAN MORALITY BE LEGISLATED?

All worthy legislation must be in harmony with the moral laws of the universe which God has established. This means that the laws of the Land must be morally based, and they must be designed to preserve and perpetuate moral acts by judging immoral ones.

The issue of morality is germane to the basic function of government – the protection of life and property. Every issue before every legislature in the nation. State and Federal, is at base a moral issue. Every law that is made should help to preserve a moral climate in which citizens may pursue their legitimate interests without being plundered or otherwise victimized by anti-moral forces.

CONSERVATISM

If by "conservative" is meant a commitment to the conservation of biblical and constitutional principles, the conservative movement is a constructive force in America. To an alarming degree, America has strayed away from her founding principles and has witnessed the development of supergovernment and the secular-humanist state. We need to rediscover, restore and conserve the legitimate founding principles of this nation.

DEFENSE

The very first obligation of our government is to protect the lives and property of our citizens.

We are confronted with an unprecedented national emergency, a crisis of survival. The outcome will be either the victory of freedom under God or the destruction or enslavement of our people.

Just as God led Nehemiah to rebuild the defensive wall around Jerusalem, thus establishing the biblical principle of national defense, we must arise and rebuild the defensive wall of America that is broken down. At the same time we must humble ourselves, seek the face of God, turn from our wicked ways, and pray earnestly for peace.

HUMANISM

There are only two movements in history – God's and man's. God's movement is revealed in the Holy Scriptures, which tell us about salvation through Christ, truth, freedom, morality, justice, love and the life of service.

Man's movement is humanism. It denies the Word of God as the reliable guide for the life of man on earth. It is a godless, groundless secular religion whose adherents worship at the shrine of man. It represents man's best effort to shape his society apart from God.

Humanism pervades education, government, and our society in general today. It must be counteracted, not with the sword but the Gospel and the faithful application of the Word of God in all areas of life in America.

FREE ENTERPRISE

Free Enterprise is freedom in the economic dimension of life. The Bible clearly establishes private property (Exodus 20:15, 17; Deuteronomy 27:17), which is basic to the free economy. Responsible stewardship of property and of talent is expected of God's people, as is diligence and integrity in the rendering of services.

Capitalism involves the private ownership of the means of production. Unlike socialism-communism (state ownership of the means of production) and Fascism-Naziism (state control of the means of production), capitalism provides for freedom of savings, investment, labor and enterprise, without intervention by government except for restraint of crime.

Capitalism is the opposite of the government-controlled economy, and is the only system which harmonizes with a Biblical viewpoint. Whatever defects are ascribed to capitalism are minimal in comparison with those of the opposite systems, the fruits of which are evident in Poland and other socialist-bloc states today.

RACIAL MINORITIES

God loves all people alike, and our Lord Jesus Christ died for all. No race is superior to another. Members of all races are equally responsible to live in society as good citizens, and should be judged equally under the law for all offenses. "He that justifieth the wicked, and he that condemneth the just, even they both are an abomination to the Lord" (Proverbs 17:15).

Jobs and wages should be based on merit, regardless of race. No member of a racial minority should expect favored treatment on the basis of race, and no member of a racial majority should extend unfavorable treatment on the basis of race.

EVOLUTION

The theory that the universe developed from chance beginnings, and that man evolved from lower forms of life, is spiritually, morally, intellectually and scientifically bankrupt. It makes no provision for the most basic observable fact of our physical universe – that every effect must have a cause, and that the cause must be greater than the effect.

The scientific superiority of creation as the explanation of the origin of the universe and of all life has been asserted by many of the greatest scientists. The Bible teaches that the existence and power of God is clearly discernible in the physical universe (Romans 1:19-20).

The entire moral fabric of America has been affected adversely by the false teaching in our public schools that man is but an animal with no responsibility to the Living God, whose existence is denied.

The view that God created the universe and man is more than an article of faith; it is scientifically superior and should be presented in all tax-supported institutions of learning. Offered side-by-side with all other explanations of life, the creationist concept will prevail.

APPENDIX B

PURPOSE OF THE STATE ROUNDTABLE ORGANIZATION

The purpose of the State Roundtable is to provide education, information and direction for leaders concerned with moral issues at the national, state and local levels, establishing effective lines of communication with citizens of diverse faiths and denominations who desire to work for the furtherance of the following ten-point program:

1. Provide a forum for the exchange of information and ideas among pastors, organizational leaders and laymen on matters of public interest.

2. Foster spiritual leadership through recognition of basic Biblical principles, and application of these Biblical principles to American life.

3. Serve as a clearinghouse and provide information to churches, spiritual leaders and other organizations on issues related to family, moral, and other public concerns.

4. Further the knowledge and understanding of the citizens of the United States as relating to Biblical responsibility in government.

5. Engage in non-partisan research and analysis for the benefit of the general public on family, moral, and other issues involved in governmental matters.

6. Prepare and disseminate educational material and conduct educational activities in support of the general purposes of the corporation.

7. Conduct and sponsor forums, lectures, debates and similar programs.
8. Assist other charitable, educational and social organizations in the conduct of similar activities.
9. Establish in the headquarters office and/or elsewhere, all departments and activities necessary to carry out the purposes of the corporation.
10. Encourage by precept and example an utter dependence on God through intercessory prayer.

The end-result of a properly functioning State Roundtable will be the extension of this ten-fold program throughout the particular state, with local Roundtable chapters effectively carrying out these vital functions in as many cities, towns and communities as possible statewide. All individuals and groups concerned will be involved in developing programs consistent with the existing commonality of attitude and language relative to the moral issues confronting the nation. They will also exhibit a cooperative relationship in dealing with these issues constructively and successfully.

APPENDIX C

(Here is the original mission statement of The Roundtable that Ed McAteer founded in 1979. At its height of operation, over one million homes were on its mailing list. Additionally are listed The Roundtable's Directors and Council of '56.)

THE PRIORITY

Many years ago, as David stood and viewed the valley wherein victory or defeat would be brought to God's people Israel, he cried, "Is there not a cause?" When Goliath roared, the dismayed and fearful army only saw how impossible the odds were. But David wasn't bothered by the giant's size. Goliath (like the diabolical forces of communism today) was defying the living God. "The battle is the Lord's!"

God is looking for men who will "stand in the gap" for America. The Scripture declares, "When the enemy shall come in like a flood, the Spirit of the Lord shall lift up a standard – morality and righteousness – but He uses men to accomplish His purpose.

The last paragraph of the Declaration of Independence states: "We mutually pledge to each other our lives, our fortunes, and our sacred honor." The gallant fifty-six who made that promise knew they were risking everything. If they won the fight, the best they could expect would be years of hardship in a struggling new nation. And if they lost…they would face a hangman's rope as traitors.

These were men of means, well educated and cultured. Twenty-four were lawyers and jurists. Eleven were merchants; nine were farmers and owners of large plantations. But they signed the pledge and paid the price…and freedom was born.

If those 56 men were willing to risk everything in order to give birth to freedom, can we do any less to preserve it in our generation? God is looking for men of courage and moral fiber, men like:

Patrick Henry who said: "Is life so dear or peace so sweet as to be purchased at the price of chains or slavery? Forbid it, almighty God! I know not what course others may take; but as for me, give me liberty, or give me death."

John Paul Jones fought as if the whole cause of American liberty depended on him alone. It was September in 1779 when the British asked if he would surrender. His reply: " I have not yet begun to fight!"

John Stark, one of the Green Mountain boys, was told before the Battle of Bennington that the hill could not be taken. He growled back, "I'll take that hill before sundown, or Molly Stark's a widow."

On the green at Lexington, in the snow at Valley Forge, on the fields of Gettysburg, the waters of the Marne, the beaches of Normandy and the sands of Iwo Jim…a million and more of our countrymen have died for my freedom. They did not die in vain. I am an American, and my country is their eternal monument to freedom. And we too, all of us together, must stand and be counted.

If we don't say it, no voice will. If we don't believe it, no one will. If we don't dream it, no heart will. If we don't build it, no hands will. Love it with all your might. Support it with all your faith. Defend it with all your life.

Yours, in the cause that counts,

Edward E. McAteer
President

"Righteousness... exalteth a nation."

Born and built upon basic principles of righteousness, the United States has been blessed in her short 200- year history as no other nation.

America has a heritage that cries, "We cannot go without God..."

- The right to life, liberty and the pursuit of happiness originated with God.
- The signers of the Declaration of Independence avowed firm reliance on the protection of Divine providence.

"Sin is a reproach to any people..."

MORALITY

- Drug abuse. Over 400,000 heroin addicts in the U.S. (60,000 in California alone). Twenty-two million Americas smoke marijuana.
- Alcoholism. The number one drug and health problem. Over 9 million alcoholics in the U.S. Retail sales of alcohol in one recent year totaled 32.5 billion dollars.
- Homosexuality. There is currently proposed legislation that prohibits employment discrimination on the basis of sexual orientation (i.e. male or female homosexuals, bisexuals or heterosexuals.)
- Pornography. The U.S. will soon be the porno capital of the world.

CRIME

- Crime cost the taxpayer 2 billion dollars a year. In the past ten years, violent crimes have increased 174% in America. Murder is up 129%. Aggravated assault is up 139%. A serious crime is committed every 3.5 seconds. One robbery is committed every 83 seconds. One murder is committed every 27 seconds.
- George Washington prayed that God would keep the United States in His Holy protection.
- Abraham Lincoln, in the Gettysburg Address, declared that our nation was indeed under God.
- "In God We Trust" adorns our money.

During the past few decades America has forsaken God. As a nation we have turned away from Him and have given our souls to secular humanism.

FAMILY

- Divorce rate in America is now 46%. In two major cities, there were more divorces than marriages. As of 1978. 1.2 million couples (doubling the 1970 number) were living together.
- Child Abuse. Two thousand American children die annually from child abuse (over 70% from stepfathers –the result of divorce).
- Abortion. Each day over 4,000 unborn babies are destroyed by abortion (over 1 million annually).

MILITARY

During the past 10 years of disarmament talks, Russia has converted a U.S. advantage in 1969 of nearly 2-to-1 in strategic launchers, to a Soviet advantage. Unless drastic changes are urgently made in our defenses, the Soviet Union might coerce the United States into a total surrender.

The fact is that we cannot survive as a free nation unless we alter the course we have followed at breakneck speed for the past five decades. Something must be done.

PARTICIPATION PLAN

The Roundtable has one focus – public policy concerning moral issues. Moral change is not an option, but an absolute necessity if western civilization and the Judeo-Christian ethics upon which it has been based are to survive. The Roundtable is not a collaborating force of leaders for a denomination, theological, ecumenical, or partisan political view. It is a coalition of dedicated national leaders who have one concern – the moral rebirth of America. The Roundtable has become the vanguard and national voice of other morality-oriented organizations and also maintains a separate structure of its own. The Roundtable solicits the participation of all those in the nation who affirm a Biblically-rooted moral viewpoint relative to:

- American Family
- Decency in Television Programming
- Gay Rights
- Freedom of Worship
- Pornography
- Abortion
- Child Abuse

THE FUNCTION OF THE ROUNDTABLE IS TWOFOLD:

EDUCATIONAL

"My people are destroyed for lack of knowledge" (Hosea 4:6). Too long have we gullibly relied on the news media, leftist "think tanks" and misdirected political leaders to supply us with accurate information. Consequently, many faithful citizens in our country are unfamiliar with the personnel and workings of our political system. That is why education is vital. The moral community must have:

1. In-depth information on a consistent basis about government activities.
2. Analysis of issues and events, presented by professionals sympathetic to pro-family and pro-God concerns.
3. Contact with elected officials and representatives of national organizations.
4. The resources to effectively present the position of the moral community.

The Roundtable will meet those needs through the following means:

- National Affairs Briefings
- National Leadership Seminars
- Single-Issue Rallies
- Cassette Tapes
- Publications
- Media Appearances
- Personal Appearances

LEADERSHIP

God works through leaders and is looking for those who will "stand in the gap" (II Chronicles 16:9) and provide courageous leadership. These leaders will provide influence, not only for their own constituency, but for local and national public policies. The planned implementation of this program is:

The Roundtable will sponsor public meetings in Washington, D.C. and in other key cities. Prominent leaders of national organizations will conduct seminars for Roundtable participants and present reports on issues of concern to the group.

The State Roundtable organizations operating in all fifty states will cooperate in organizing these events. In some instances elected officials at the state and federal levels will share their own special insights relative to public policy.

PURPOSE

1. Provide a forum for exchange of information and ideas among pastors, organizational leaders and laymen on matters of public interest.
2. Foster spiritual leadership through application of basic Biblical principles to American life.
3. Serve as clearinghouse to churches, spiritual leaders and various organizations on issues relating to family, moral and other public concerns.
4. Further an understanding of Biblical responsibility in government.
5. Engage in research and analysis on family, moral and other issues, for the benefit of the general public.
6. Prepare and disseminate educational materials and con-

duct educational activities.

7. Conduct and sponsor forums, lectures, debates, briefings and conferences.
8. Assist other charitable, educational and social organizations in the conduct of similar activities.
9. Establish in the headquarters office and/or elsewhere, all departments and activities necessary to carry out the purposes of the corporation.
10. Encourage by precept and example an utter dependence on God through intercessory prayer.

PARTNERS

Original Board of Directors

Mrs. James Augustine
Memphis, TN

Mr. John Beckett
Elyia, OH

Mr. J.W. Bell
Memphis, TN

Mr. Curtis Brunk
Denver, CO

Mr. K.Q. Chedester
La Follette, TN

Miss Nancy DeMoss
Bryn Mar, PA

Mr. Daniel Dil
Los Angeles, CA

Rev. Del Fehsenfield, Jr.
Buchannan, MI

Dr. Robert Hackman
Murfreesboro, TN

Mr. William Ham
Memphis, TN

Mr. Richard Headrick
Laurel, Ms

Dr. E.V. Hill
Los Angeles, CA

Dr. Richard Hogue
Edmond, Ok

Mr. Nelson Bunker Hunt
Dallas, TX

Dr. D. James Kennedy
Ft. Lauderdale, FL

Mr. Ben Marshall
Memphis, TN

E. E. McAteer
Memphis, TN

Mr. Stanley McCay
Baldwyn, MS

Dr. Paige Patterson
Dallas, TX

Dr. James Robison
Ft. Worth, TX

Mr. D.G. Seago
West Memphis, AR

Rep. Mark Siljander
Three Rivers, MI

Mr. Thomas Singleton
Nashville, TN

Dr. Charles F. Stanley
Atlanta, GA

Mr. Jack Stewart
Morristown, TN

Mr. Michael Valerio
Boston, MA

Max Williams
Memphis, TN

Roundtable State Directors

Tom Sizemore
Montgomery, AL

Arne Halverson
Ketchikan, AK

Tim McAteer
Maumelle, AR

E. Ray Moore, Jr.
W. Lafayette, IN

Vernard Whattoff
Ames, IO

Jim Jeffries, Jr.
Lenexa, KS

John Pellin
Syracuse, NE

Don Gustavason
Carson City, NV

Michael S. McCarthy
Branchville, NJ

Ron Zielinski
LaHabra, CA

Doug Kreiger
Denver, CO

Daniel Mariano
Norwalk, CT

Mrs. Winifred Spence
Odessa, DE

Jim Harkins
Ft. Walton Beach, FL

Bill Powell
Buchanan, GA

Jimmy Prieto
Honolulu, HI

Edwin Allen Smith
Riggins, ID

Don Lyon
Rockford, IL

David Proffitt
Knoxville, TN

Tom Kimbell
Houston, TX

Earl Blackburn
Provo, UT

Rev. Richard Oldham
Bowling Green, KY

Jim Thornton
Jonesville, LA

Ray Paine
Livermore, ME

Bill Comfort
Stevensville, MD

Tom Dewey
Dedham, ME

Robert Bradford, II
Minneapolis, MN

Roland Byrd
Louisville, MS

Robert Gladstone
Ellisville, MO

Mike McGovern
Missoula, MT

Don Griffes
East Charleston, VT

Mark W. Bonds
Forest, VA

Dan Harris, Jr.
Olympia, WA

Mrs. Roger Fulton
New York, NY

Richard C. Titus
Raleigh, NC

Rev. John Wall
Grand Forks, ND

Jay Menafee
Newbury, OH

Marilyn Hogue
Edmond, OK

Dr. Claude Pike
Oregon City, OR

Don Kauffman
Lancaster, PA

Orin Briggs
Columbia, SC

Lindell Howard
Mitchell, SD

Rod Mays
St. Albans, WV

Frank Tamel
Oak Creek, WI

Council of "56"
Hon. Larry P. McDonald 1935-1983

Mr. Jerry Armstrong
Abilene, TX

Mr. Richard Ford
Dallas, TX

Dr. William Marshner
Front Royal, VA

Rev. Raymond Barber
Ft. Worth, TX

Dr. George Benson
Search, AR

Mrs. Marjorie Cambell
Wilton, CT

Mr. John Cansler
Greenville, TN

Mr. Clay Claiborne
San Antonio, TX

Rev. Walter Cosby
Louisville, KY

Dr. W. A. Criswell
Dallas, TX

Mrs. Mary Crowley
Dallas, TX

Mr. Rafael Cruz
Houston, TX

Miss Louise Dunagan
Memphis, TN

Dick & Shirley Ellis
Wilmington, OH

Dr. Jerry Falwell
Lynchburg, VA

Rev. Charles Fiore
Madison, WI

Mr. John Fisher
Boston, MA

Mr. Charles Fitzgerald
Murfreesboro, TN

Rev. Greer Garrott
Memphis, TN

Sen. Jesse Helms
Washington, D.C.

Mr. Melvin Hodges
Baton Rouge, LA

Hon. James Jeffries
Kansas City, KS

Dr. Mildred F. Jefferson
Boston, MA

Mr. Woody Jenkins
Baton Rouge, LA

Mr. George Jones
Memphis, TN

Rev. Russ Kaemmerling
Dallas, TX

Gen. George Keegan, Jr.
Arlington, VA

Mr. H. E. Kirtland
LaGrange, TN

Gen. Albion Knight
Bethesda, MD

Dr. Tim LaHaye
Washington, D. C.

Mr. Marshall Larkins
Clinton, KY

Dr. James Latimer
Memphis, TN

Mr. James Lofton
Middleton, TN

Dr. Bobby Moore
Memphis, TN

Mr. William J. Murray
Austin, TX

Dr. Gary North
Tyler, TX

Mr. Larry Parrish
Memphis, TN

Mr. Bobby Robertson
Sumter, SC

Mr. Tom Riner
Louisville, KY

Mr. F. D. Sadler
Memphis, TN

Dr. Robert Spoede
Dayton, TN

Mrs. Helen Marie Taylor
Richmond, VA

Mr. William Taylor
Louisville, MS

Dr. Earl E. Whitwell
Tupelo, MS

Mr. Tom Wicker
Friendsville, TN

Miss Kim Wickes
W. Memphis, AR

Dr. J. C. Wilke
Cincinnati, OH

THE POWER OF ONE

The Ed McAteer Story

To order additional copies of "The Power of One" for friends, complete this form and send it with payment (check or money order) of $16.95. Quantity prices available upon request. Books will be sent post paid.

Name_______________________________________

Address ____________________________________

City______________________ State______ Zip_________

Phone (   ) ______________________________

Email_______________________________________

SEND TO:
Dan Johnson
PO Box 341841, Memphis, TN 38184
dejsr@bellsouth.net
1-800-216-4333
Make checks payable to Dan Johnson.